Therapy FOR THE Wounded Child

Therapy FOR THE Wounded Child

Silent Wounds Scream for Attention

JERRY W. ROBINSON, MAC

Charleston, SC

www.PalmettoPublishing.com

Therapy for the Wounded Child:
Silent Wounds Scream for Attention

Copyright © 2021 by Jerry W. Robinson, M.A.C.

August 2021

1209 Alnwick Lane

Saginaw, TX 76131

All Scripture is from the New American Standard Bible unless otherwise indicated.[1]

First Edition

Hardcover: 978-1-68515-348-9

Paperback: 978-1-68515-349-6

eBook: 978-1-68515-350-2

Steve

Dr. G. and Jerry

CONTENTS

FOREWORD

By Dr. Robert L. Gilliam
Ed.D., Ph.D., LPC-S, L.C.P.C., C.S.C., Ord. Min.
Executive Director of Dayspring Counseling, Irving, Texas

At least twenty years ago, God saw fit to interface my ministry and Jerry Robinson's ministry. God used an unusual instrument as His tool for this union, a unique gathering known as Little Flock, whose motto was, "Not for everybody, but for anybody!" This was usually followed by an equally odd invitation to their Bible study, namely, "You are welcome, warts and all."

Initially, eight brave souls gathered because they had been injured or rejected in some religious setting or just did not seem to fit anywhere else at the time. When our total attendance reached one hundred, we became a Bonafide Mission. A few months later, we were a full-fledged church, with a faith-based professional counseling center housed in the same relatively small facility. It was amid these modest conditions that God set the stage for this publication's narrative and coordinated the real-life experiences from which its storyline emerged.

I was the pastor of Little Flock and the executive director of Dayspring Counseling Center, its co-ministry. Jerry Robinson and his wife, Jan, became active members, as various aspects of their ministry began to bloom in several directions, in keeping with the admonition of 1 Peter 4:11: "If any man minister, let him do it as of the ability (or abilities) that God giveth." And he did, and they did, and I respected the array of gifts and ministering abilities that God so endowed and fostered!

As brother Jerry has aptly confirmed, this book's characters and contents are truly biography-based, reflecting our real experiences during those impressive formative and reformative years. Therefore, it is my pleasure to go on record here as officially endorsing this book, including its descriptions of the counseling and ministerial approaches described herein. As a professional counseling therapist with three doctorates and seven licenses in related fields, I can confirm that Jerry's testimonies are accurate accounts of his growth and development.

Finally, we have guaranteed (and still guarantee) that any suggestions, ideas, or recommendations we share meet two criteria: 1) They will be biblically compatible, and 2) they will be psychologically sound. That combination means that they are as sure to work as any of God's laws of nature. It also explains the continued impact of this ministry.

John G. Digel

jgd045@comcast.net

I first met Jerry Robinson in January 2010 at Northshore Baptist Church, Kirkland, WA. I still remember the first time I met Jerry. I was nervous about sharing my grief with him, but his peaceful, listening presence immediately put me at ease. He walked with me through the period of my pain and suggested ways to transfer my grief to Jesus. Jerry listened and provided me spiritual guidance, and I realize now what a great blessing God bestowed on me in placing Jerry in my life.

During his ministry, he revealed to me the work he had been involved with through Wycliffe in Papua New Guinea, which helped deal with my pain. I developed a lifelong love for missionary work from listening to Jerry's stories.

In 2016, Jerry asked me if I would read his rough draft of this book. I learned that Jerry's present self did not exist until after God healed him through Dr. Gilliam's counseling. God worked miracles in Jerry's life, removing the bricks and walls he had built up due to his childhood experiences. Jerry's healing shows the power of our Lord and Savior. Jesus answered Jerry's prayers to transform him into the man he was created to be by God.

The Jerry Robinson I know today is a new creation. God, the master potter, took apart the "old Jerry" and recreated him into the person he is today. I pray that this book will help many others to seek help in dealing with the difficulty of raising a family while serving in the missionary field.

—John Digel

Meet Dark Pony, me, Jerry Wayne Robinson. I have a B.S. degree from Dallas Bible College in Bible and Missions and a M.A.C. degree from Western Seminary Seattle. My wife and I live in Saginaw, Texas, north of Fort Worth. My wife Jan and I have two grown children, Steve and Wendy. We were missionaries with the Wycliffe Bible Translators doing literacy work with the Weri and Rawa tribes in Papua New Guinea for twenty years.

I witnessed Weri and Rawa lives under much stress, their happy times, and their sorrows. I learned that life's simple things do not clutter their days and that generosity is highly valued. The mark of a true leader was his ability to interact with anyone.

All pretense of wrong motives quickly vanished when my entire world, and all that I touched, collapsed in a single hour. I believe my story will encourage people to seek help when they are faced with an impossible barrier and do not know what to do, just as Steve and I experienced. I am so thankful for the Summer Institute of Linguistics-Papua New Guinea (SIL-PNG) leaders for sending us to the USA to get help. I am happy we can look back on all that happened and see where God worked things out for us, and we became emotionally healthy.

You, the reader, will join me in the counseling process as an observer, the fly on the wall. I waive my right to privacy as you witness Dr. Sydney and I interact. My purpose in doing this is to remove the mystery surrounding the counseling process and recognize the importance of seeking help. I am living proof that counseling works, and help is available. I let God do His work in me, changing me into who I am today.

What happens in a counseling session? You will observe the therapist at work with an emotionally wrecked client: me. He provides me skills to become emotionally healthy. The reader will learn the concept of Reparenting the Inner Child, and Landmarks, Boundaries, and Walls, that are distinctively Dr. Gilliam's and have been tested for over forty years with a high success rate.

I have written about my son, Steve, and me coming home from Papua New Guinea, and about the hour that changed our lives forever. Rarely do missionary children talk about what it is like growing up on the mission field and having a workaholic father who puts his work first and family last. Seldom do you read of an absentee dad who admits his lack of leadership and uses his job to hide his insecurities, and even less frequently do you learn of its effects on himself and his family and his work. But here, in *Therapy for the Wounded Child,* I share all of that and more.

I could not tell this story without permission from Steve. He said yes, I had his okay to author our story. "The best therapy for an emotionally wounded child is for him to witness a positive change in his parents." -Dr. Dan Allender. We damage our children with our negative attitudes more than we will ever know.

I wish you well on your journey through these pages, Jerry

CHAPTER 1

The Hour My Dreams Died

Echoes from a Wounded Child

On November 24, 1991, a Sunday, I was enjoying a delicious dinner with my brother Yunu Siwi and his family when we heard the Wycliffe helicopter approaching. I thought this strange. The mission did not fly on Sundays, and why was it coming here to Tauta? I planned to return to the mission center after dinner by public transport, a three-hour ride.

The village children ran to the abandoned airstrip to meet the chopper, and they escorted the pilot to find me. At that point we had been with the Rawa people for seven years and eleven months.

That was the hour that changed my entire world, turning all I cherished into confusion and panic. I went out to meet the pilot. He said there was a family emergency, and I needed to go with him immediately; there was no time to return to my house for any belongings. I said goodbye to Yunu and left with the pilot. (The flying time between Ukarumpa, our mission center, and Tauta was fifteen minutes.)

The mission director met me at the airfield and drove me to my neighbor's house. He did not tell me what was happening, just saying my family needed me. My wife, Jan, and our daughter, Wendy, met me in the yard, sobbing. The director would not let me go into our home, and I did not see Steve, our teenage son. When they finally spoke, their news left me in shock, and I could not think. I had no time to blame God. I was numb.

∞∞∞

Gerry DeYoung, a coworker, knocked the knife from Steve's hand, then held him in a fatherly embrace to comfort him. When the police took Steve to jail, Gerry stayed with him all night long, embracing him in his love. I wanted to say thank you for being there for Steve when I was to upset to be the father he needed. I knew he needed love, not punishment.

Someone paid for the chartered helicopter trip to Tauta to get me and bring me home to Ukarumpa. Someone comforted Jan and Wendy and protected them from experiencing the chaotic mess Steve made inside our home. Many people cleaned up most of the trashed house before I arrived. Someone paid for and replaced all the glass for the broken windows. Someone booked the flight from our mission center in Ukarumpa to Dallas, Texas. Someone called ahead to arrange for Steve to be admitted to the hospital. Someone helped Jan and Wendy as they tried to pack and join Steve and me in the U.S.A. Someone flew with us in case there were problems during the flight. So many people helped us with all these things. We do not know who you are, but God does. To all these someone's, I sincerely thank you.

With arrangements completed for Steve and me to leave Papua New Guinea, the next morning we caught an early flight to Port Moresby, the capital city. From there we flew directly to Dallas Fort Worth airport. Leaders from the Wycliffe headquarters met us and drove us to Richardson, Texas, to the Minirth-Meier Clinic. Steve was immediately committed to treatment for extreme depression and a battery of tests.

God used sickness and family issues to get my attention. I had neglected my family in my work for Him, and I did not realize how that can affect the whole family. Steve had a nervous breakdown, and we had to get help immediately. God went before us and prepared each step of the way. Our Wycliffe leaders mandated all the family to receive counseling and be released with good health before we could return to our work. It took me six years to get healthy.

I felt like a flower yanked from the ground and tossed away. We missed the dedication of the Rawa New Testament on September 12, 1992. Our supporting churches did not want to sponsor home-assigned missionaries, so our monthly finances dropped below the amount required for our ministry in Papua New Guinea.

I spiraled into a deep depression and doubted God's goodness. The strain on my marriage neared the breaking point. I had lost my career and my friends and my purpose for living. As if that were not enough, I began to remember childhood trauma.

CHAPTER 2

Required Counseling

The Starting Point[2,3]

The starting point for me is to find a therapist who fits well with my expectations. Arrange to get their Disclosure Statement. This document contains their qualifications and the style of therapy they practice. After evaluating it, I either proceed to enroll or keep looking for the right fit. Wycliffe had its own counseling department, but I did not fit there. I found Irving Christian Counseling. The agency agreed to work with me on a sliding scale as my insurance was limited for therapy. The first session is complimentary with some therapists; this is the time to size each other up and decide whether the counselor and you are a good fit. You sign the Authorization to Work Together; this will be duplicated—one copy for you and one for the counselor.

The following therapy account is fiction, but the scenarios are realistic. Dr. Sydney and Mountain Brook Institute for Training and Development are fiction but are based on Dr. Gilliam and the Dayspring Counseling Services and Dayspring Institute for Training and Development.

Meet Dr. Sydney, my therapist[4]
A family friend posing as Dr. Sydney

Dr. Joseph E. Sydney,
ED.D., H.D., L.C.P.C., C.S.C.,
License # LC00037222
9809 N 124th Street, Suite 306, Dallas, TX 75034
DR.J.E.K.@gmail.com

Your Fundamental Rights as a Client[5]

As my client, you have the right to know my qualifications, how I work, and what you can expect from me as your counselor. After reading my disclosure information, you can choose to work with me or not.

You have the right to understand my reasons for making suggestions or using particular procedures. I will try to explain these clearly, but if you have any questions, please ask me.

You have the right to refuse to do anything I suggest.

You have the right to stop counseling with me at any time for any reason.

Everything you share with me is in the strictest confidence.

If you tell me you will harm yourself or someone else, the law requires me to do anything I can to prevent that.

If you contemplate or commission a crime or harmful act, I must report this.

Suppose you are a minor (under twenty-one years of age), and the information acquired by me indicates you were a victim or subject of a crime. In that case, I may testify fully upon any examination, trial, or other proceedings in which the crime commission is the inquiry subject.

You waive your confidentiality if you bring charges against me.

Regarding a subpoena by the court, the warrant only relates to the complaint or report.

Your written consent is required for me to disclose confidential communications to others.

The purpose of the law regulating counselors is:[6]

A. To protect public health and safety.

B. To empower the citizens of the state of Texas by submitting a complaint process against those counselors who would commit acts of unprofessional conduct.

Counselors practicing counseling for a fee must be registered or certified with the Department of Health to protect public health and safety.[7]

Registration of an individual with the Department of Health does not include recognizing any practice standards, nor necessarily imply any treatment's effectiveness.

My Credentials and Work Experience:[8]

Dr. Joseph E. Sydney, Ed.D., Ph.D., LPC-S, L.C.P.C., C.S.C.
Executive Director, Mountain Brook Institute for Training and Development

Dr. Sydney is the ultimate blend of extensive professional training, holding numerous licenses and certifications, with many years of successful practice and experience. He has a warm, personal, down-to-earth manner of relating and communicating. All these qualifications reflect an underlying God-given therapeutic skill set and a deep sense of ministry.

Dr. Sydney holds a bachelor's degree in Bible and Education, a master's degree in Counseling and Guidance, and three doctorates in related fields of counseling. He is a licensed professional counselor, a licensed clinical pastoral counselor, and a certified school counselor, C.S.C. He is State Board approved to supervise counselor interns in Continuing Education for Licensed Professional Counselors.

As Mountain Brook's executive director, he counsels individuals, couples, families, and groups. About half of his clients are dealing with issues related to marriage, family, or parenting. The other half, says Dr. Sydney, includes almost every issue you can think of and a few things you probably wouldn't think of! Other counselors refer their more complicated cases to Dr. Sydney.

Dr. Sydney often speaks at seminars, conferences, retreats, churches, and professional meetings. He uses music, humor, metaphors, and homespun illustrations efficiently in his counseling. He has authored several books and workbooks and has composed musical selections, most of which have therapeutic implications.

When people seek counseling, it is because they want something to be different in their lives. They want to change their life situations, solve a particular problem, or decide or understand what is happening in their lives or within themselves.[9]

For counseling to be most effective, you must commit time and energy and participate in the process. Most counseling sessions are for fifty minutes each. The number of sessions needed varies with each person and problem.

CHAPTER 3

The Counseling Process

D_{R.} S_{YDNEY}: Once I understand your concerns, we will discuss the number of sessions you might need. The first session is complimentary. My usual model for therapy is the concept of the Inner Child, and Landmarks, Boundaries, and Walls.[10] The Inner Child model helps me systematically and uniquely identify your core issues, internal self-talk, and identify the origin of these, whether the self-talk is negative or positive. The negatives we will counter with truth. This entire process is to determine your belief system. After this, I use the Landmarks, Boundaries, and Walls model to identify healthy relationships and correct the inappropriate, damaged ones. I want to visualize with you a healthy you.

Inner-child therapy is based on the premise that people struggle emotionally because they have unresolved childhood issues. In this psychotherapy method, the therapist guides the client through an in-depth exploration of childhood traumatic events and directs the client in reworking the associated disturbing emotions.

These are the steps we will follow for your recovery:

- To find your inner child and help him grow up.

- To work on his negative self-talk and replace that with positive self-talk.

- To work on his belief system.

- To work on the lies he believes.

- To work on ways to reparent him.

- To find your landmarks, boundaries, walls (L.B.W.).

- To set and reset L.B.W.

- To work on patterns for living.
- To identify the different boundaries.
- To determine the components of each boundary.
- To design a memory marker.

Most sessions are scheduled once a week for as long as necessary. We will start and finish on time. After our first meeting, I will adjust the schedule depending on your situation.

The healing process takes time. You cannot rush it. Some people may respond to several brief sessions, while others may need several months or years.

Homework:

Homework in counseling is informative work done outside of the meeting. It extends the length of the session and increases progress. Clients who come to see me get assigned out-of-session tasks.

There is flexibility, and other content will be added as needed.

Complimentary session: checking each other out

Dr. Sydney: Hello, Mr. Robinson. I am Dr. Sydney. Please have a seat here by the door. May I get you something to drink, coffee or water? I am a Christian, and I believe in prayer and the power of God. Do you have any objection if I pray and ask God to give wisdom in helping you accomplish a healthy relationship with yourself, with others, and with God?

Jerry: Please call me Jerry. I, too, am a Christian and appreciate you praying for me. This whole counseling process is terrifying me, and I am nervous. Sharing my emotions is something I seldom do.

Dr. Sydney: Heavenly Father, thank you for bringing Jerry here. As we work together, may the Holy Spirit give us wisdom, the courage to face the hard things in life, and comfort, love, joy, peace, and healing. In Jesus's name, amen.

When you called the office for counseling, the receptionist mailed you the packet with my credentials and treatment plan. At times I may take notes or record our sessions to help me remember details. Do you have any questions regarding my credentials or your rights as a client?

JERRY: No.

DR. SYDNEY: I want to walk you through the counseling process:[11]

1. What counseling is;

2. Common misconceptions about counseling;

3. What individual counseling is;

4. Tips on how to make the most out of individual counseling.

There are many definitions of counseling floating around, some more complicated than others. Simply, it is a way to help clients understand and clarify their views of their living space and to learn to reach their self-determined goals through meaningful, well-informed choices and the resolution of problems of an emotional or interpersonal nature.

My definition of counseling is a professional relationship that empowers diverse individuals, families, and groups to accomplish mental-health wellness, education, and career goals by providing clients with advice, which will, in turn, become a guide in making important decisions. The information by professionals known as counselors becomes the data used in the counseling session or meeting agreed upon by both parties.

People's attitudes toward counseling have changed. No longer does a person need to solve a problem. He can have therapy even if he has no specific question or problem requiring an immediate solution. Proper treatment has excellent results.

A few benefits of counseling:

- Reduce anxiety & stress/trauma resolution

- Better relationships

- Develop assertiveness

- Emotional intelligence

- Clearer academic & career goals

- Establish boundaries

- Greater self-confidence

The client becomes more self-aware, gaining in-depth insight into himself. This understanding promotes greater self-acceptance and appreciation, thus encouraging further improvement on his strengths and good points and change for the better, where necessary.

The client's values and beliefs thought to be permanent and set in stone are challenged and become more open to change, making room for flexibility, allowing them to be adaptable and adjustable to change. As a result, the person is open to altering his thoughts, behavior, and feelings.

Along with self-awareness, the client also becomes more aware of the people around him. He better understands other people: why they do what they do, what motivates them, and what is important to them. This increased sensitivity and understanding pave the way toward building and maintaining more robust relationships.

The client will be empowered to set goals and accomplish them. Counseling helps clients gain clarity and urges them to produce strategies and ideas that will let them achieve their goals.

The client's health will also benefit. Many claim that, after counseling sessions, they feel significantly lighter, and their stress levels reduce considerably.

The client obtains the opportunity to make amends for past wrongs that others have committed or forgive mistakes against him. Again, this will promote goodwill among people, and the client will have improved relations with others.

Jerry: I appreciate you explaining all that. I am new to the counseling experience and didn't know what to expect. Thank you.

Dr. Sydney: Jerry, what do you want from counseling?

Jerry: I don't know. I feel nothing is working for me. I don't know who I am or what I will do. My family is falling apart; my marriage is unstable; my teenage son had a breakdown. I cannot return to work without my counselor's written approval, as well as approval from my boss. I was a missionary with Wycliffe and was in Papua New Guinea (PNG) when my son tried to burn down our home.

Dr. Sydney: Jerry, it sounds like you are overwhelmed with everything. Can you tell me about some positive things in your life right now?

JERRY: I am married and have two children, a son born in 1975 and a daughter born in 1983. We were field workers doing literacy work with the Wycliffe Bible Translators and Summer Institute of Linguistics (WBT-SIL)[12] in Papua New Guinea when we had a family emergency. Family and health problems finally came to a head, with my son having a nervous breakdown. The Wycliffe directors required each of us to have counseling before we can return.

My wife, Jan, and our eight-year-old daughter are seeing Dr. Young for counseling. Our teenage son, Steve, is at the Minirth-Meier Clinic in Richardson, Texas, for evaluation and treatment, and I am here with you.

DR. SYDNEY: Please tell me your story. Do you mind if I video it?

JERRY: No, I don't mind.

I was born in Jacobia, Texas, on February 14, 1943. My father was a sharecropper farmer, and we lived on a cotton farm. I have five sisters and no brothers. I am next to the last in my family. I do not remember much about my life from 1943 until 1953, except that I was very lonely and insecure.

My quest for God began when I was a small child. My mother took us to the Jacobia Methodist Church each Sunday. At home, she read stories from the Bible about the famous characters and the miracles God did in their lives. She sang her favorite hymns to us in her beautiful alto voice.

I was nine years old when my family moved from Greenville to Petersburg near Lubbock, Texas. We still lived on a farm, but there were neighbors close by. For the first time in my life, I had someone my age and gender to play with. I often went to church with them. As I listened to the Sunday school teacher and the preacher, I became interested in the Bible and wanted to know God. I enjoyed hearing Bible stories and letting my imagination track them. I could visualize the people, places, and events, which made them come to life. I could see myself like some of those characters. One thing I could not imagine was being a sinner. I always thought the preacher was talking to someone else, not me! I considered myself a good boy.

God was preparing me for a personal encounter with Him, and I did not even know it. The hunger and desire to know more about Him kept growing in my heart.

By the fourth grade, I had forgotten my earlier childhood. I knew I hated life and was incredibly lonely, and that we lived on a cotton farm. But other details? Nothing. I was shy and timid and didn't have any friends. Our substitute teacher was a child molester, and some boys warned the rest of us not to stay after school to help her if we didn't want her sexually playing with us. Some weeks later, she asked me to stay and help her.

Shortly after that, I was on the playground when twin boys from my class had a piece of piano wire with them. They asked us if anyone wanted to die. We all ran away except for one girl. I watched as they killed her. She struggled and kicked for a while and then went limp, just like on TV. This was now Jerry Wayne's world.

We moved before I started fifth grade. Life on the farm was tame compared to city life. We lived in the meanest and most impoverished part of Lubbock where the cheapest houses to rent were. Mother worked in a restaurant as the pie lady, and Daddy was a security guard at a large factory. I made friends with three boys from school, Jerry S., Tommy L., and Alvin M., and the four of us remained good friends through high school.

Older boys from school were already sexually active, and they detailed their weekly conquests during recess and displayed themselves on the playground regularly. They thought it was fun to catch Jerry, Tommy, Alvin, or me, drag us over to the girls, and strip our pants off so the girls would see us naked. This shamed us to no end. They left us crying and humiliated. Complaining to the teacher did no good, nor to our parents, because they all worked and couldn't take time off to intervene. If we called the police, we'd get the reputation of being crybabies because it would go in the newspaper, and we didn't want everyone knowing we couldn't win this fight.

At the age of thirteen I began attending a little church near my home. Ms. Hufstedler taught the book of Acts in Sunday school class. I listened and asked all kinds of questions. She was always gentle and answered my questions. My curiosity was sparked, and I increasingly asked about the things of God. One evening at a church service, when the pastor invited us to come to Jesus, I realized for the first time that the call was for me and not someone else. I responded and made a public confession of my faith in Christ. Mr. and Mrs. Hufstedler were the first married couple I saw who modeled a happy marriage, and she continued to have considerable influence on my spiritual growth until her death years later.

The week before graduation from Lubbock High School, I received my draft notice from Uncle Sam, the Department of Defense, with number 24, meaning I could be drafted anytime. Wanting to avoid the Army due to claustrophobia and the Navy since I had never been on a boat, I joined the Air Force (USAF).

I was stationed at the Royal Air Force Base at Alconbury, England.[13] A highlight of my military service was meeting some servicemen who were trained by the Navigators.[14] From them, I learned to memorize Scripture, do Bible study, and lead others to Christ. On weekends we traveled to various places giving our testimonies, singing, and preaching in different churches. I went to the Holy Land with a group from another military base. I attended a Navigator's conference in Germany, and when I got back, the Great Gidding Baptist Church asked me to preach for the first time in my life. Later, an elderly missionary who had served in Borneo for forty years gave her testimony. As she spoke, I realized God was asking me to become a missionary. I look back at my three-year term in England as one of the best times of my life.

I was discharged from the USAF in December 1965 and started at Dallas Bible College (DBC) in February 1966. I enjoyed being at DBC, learning how to study the Bible and participating in all the extra ministry opportunities.

Many students didn't want to be at DBC, but their parents insisted. God gave me a ministry to nurture and encourage these students to consider the positive aspects of being there. Besides learning about God, there were good people to date! I also helped them understand their homework assignments. On Wednesday nights I preached at the Dallas Rescue Mission. Every other Sunday, my best friend and I traveled to De Queen, Arkansas, and preached at two churches, returning to Texas the same night.

One of the mission-track requirements for graduation was to spend a summer doing missionary work. I chose to go to Mexico and Central America with Practical Missionary Training (PMT). From various missionary societies I learned what missionaries do, and in the process, I had the opportunity to meet members of Wycliffe Bible Translators. Until that time, I had never considered Wycliffe as a career possibility. I feared their high academic requirements and thought I couldn't meet their standard of excellence. But the more Wycliffe missionaries I met, the more I was attracted to them.

I graduated from Dallas Bible College in 1970. That same year I applied to Wycliffe Bible Translators (WBT) and was accepted. The mission required several summers of university training in linguistics, which I took at the University of North Dakota and in Norman, Oklahoma. I then went to Mexico for Wycliffe's Jungle Camp course. After facing all the challenges of primitive life and coping well, I realized I could handle new experiences and successfully overcome challenging obstacles, which was somewhat surprising to me.

I went to PNG as a Wycliffe missionary in October 1972. In 1973 I met Jan Barker, also a missionary with Wycliffe at our main base. We were married on February 16, 1974. Our son was born in 1975, and our daughter in 1983.

We worked with the Morobe Province Weri people for six years, helping the locals prepare prep-school curriculum for beginning reading classes for children and adults. Several people from the village assisted us in preparing literacy materials. The village elders selected who they wanted me to train to teach, so I held several teacher-training workshops. I established and supervised small vernacular schools in two valleys, and I trained and managed local people in all areas of the work. After several years, I had worked myself out of a job!! Local people ran everything.

We went on a one-year leave and when we came back the teachers had stopped teaching and the elders of the villages where the school were located no longer were interested in literacy. They were caught up in the "Cargo Cult." When my family and I first arrived to help with the literacy, the elders wrongly believed we were there to assist their ancestral spirits to bring them the white man's stuff (cargo). They thought literacy was the road through which the cargo would come and when they tried that and it did not work, they stopped helping me. They were discouraged that the Scriptures did not bring them the cargo.

The Bible translators with whom we worked, Helen and Maurice Boxwell, dedicated the Weri New Testament in 1984. At that time, we moved onto a different area to work. There is no way for us to know if the schools are continuing and the Weri New Testament read.

Then, we moved to the Madang Province to work with the Rawa people in literacy and community devolvement. The Rawa Bible Translator Don Toland and his 5-year-old daughter Laurel Lynn were Best Man and Flower Girl in our wedding. We never dreamed that one day we would be working with them helping the Rawa people. We were with the Rawa people almost seven years.

In November 1991, my son had a nervous breakdown. I flew with him to Dallas for treatment at the Minirth-Meier Clinic. He was there for two months, and then he went to a residential treatment center to receive the help we could not give him. He stayed there fifteen months. Our whole family needed counseling to deal with this. Steve came home and lived with us for the last two years of high school. Upon graduation, he joined the United States Navy.

We resigned from the Wycliffe Bible Translators in July 1997, after twenty-seven years of service. I then attended Western Seminary, Seattle campus.

Wherever God puts me, I want to serve Him. He has equipped me with natural and spiritual gifts. I am gentle, friendly, dependable, accountable, thorough, warm, analytical, and a good listener. I have common sense. I have the spiritual gifts of encouragement, preaching, teaching, and helps.

The Gospel impacted my life in such a variety of ways. Reflecting, I see places where I could see nothing good, yet now I am amazed to see the very presence of God in those dark spots. God was even there during those forgotten years. I want to integrate what I have learned and am still learning with my ongoing understanding of the Gospel.

CHAPTER 4

SESSIONS 1–12

The Root of the Problem

SESSION 1—INTRODUCTION

Dr. Sydney: Hello, Jerry. May I get you something to drink, coffee, tea, or cold water?

Jerry: Yes, thank you, I will have water.

Dr. Sydney: Let us pray. Heavenly Father, thank you for bringing Jerry back. Help me to be sensitive to his needs and go at his pace. Calm his nerves and give him wisdom and understanding to reparent his inner child, which is work we will do. In the name of Jesus, amen.

There is one piece of business we need to do before we begin our work. The law requires us to sign a consent-for-therapy agreement for working together.[15] Please sign this; then I sign; you keep the top copy. Thanks.

We cannot rush the counseling process. Our final goal is to become healthy emotionally and have the skills to continue living as you desire. This is how we will approach our work:

1. We are laying the groundwork for uncovering the root of your problems. We will be dealing with the invisible part of you: thoughts, personality, and how your genetics and culture influenced these. I want you to have a good foundation of who the invisible part of you is before moving into the belief system that governs what you think about yourself and how you relate with other people.

19

2. Then we introduce you to the inner child and reparent him.

3. Once we have reparented your inner child, we will move on to the invisible barriers that separate you from everyone else.

JERRY: When I was small, everyone called me Jerry Wayne. Living life as Jerry Wayne was confusing. Nothing made sense. As Little Jerry Wayne, I had no dream of the future, as if I were a blank slate. My family would not let me make decisions. They told me I wasn't smart and that I was a liar. Grandpa Robinson placed a curse on me, saying, "That boy will never amount to anything."

Until recently I had no memories of my childhood. I lived a life that didn't allow Little Jerry Wayne to exist. And then I began to remember. To me, Jerry Wayne was the kid with a bruised background that could still hurt me after fifty years, and he mostly stayed hidden, buried in my subconscious. I was glad not to remember, because when I did, it knocked my socks off. Being overwhelmed, I became depressed, had no desire to live, and thought of suicide many times. By this time, I was in counseling.

When I was four years old, I could no longer sit in Mother's lap because I now had a baby sister who had that privilege. That was the age when my sexual abuse and daily whippings began. I hated life. Many times, I wished I were someone else.

Steve made a profession of faith in Jesus when he was five years old. Looking back, I believe Steve thought like me when the most severe things were happening in his life. His world crumbled about the time Wendy was born. Jan had morning sickness most days and couldn't give Steve the attention he needed. I also stopped giving Steve what he needed and presumed Jan would fill that gap for me. I was wrong. Before, he was the center of our family life, so he resented his sister from the beginning. I stopped playing Legos with Steve as often, and I became a workaholic, doing God's work. I did not provide a safe place for Jan or Steve. I didn't even have a safe place for myself and avoided my responsibilities at home.

Jan or I would ask Steve to do something, and he would promptly forget, so we waited and then asked again. It was as if he hadn't heard us the first two times. I wrongly thought he was choosing to disobey. It wasn't until years later that we learned Steve had attention deficit disorder (ADD). I remember seeing the same hurt in his eyes that I had as a child.

I have often wished I could turn back the clock and undo the harm to our relationship.

I thought of my life as a puzzle but without a picture to guide me while trying to put it together. Each piece was similar in shape, but I couldn't tell the border pieces because they were not straight edged. The colors were dull and bland. God is the one who takes each person's life and puts it together, adding lots of vibrant colors. I will have to wait to see my puzzle completed by Him.

DR. SYDNEY: I look forward to our time together. Let's plan to meet three times a week on Mondays, Wednesdays, and Fridays at 10:00 a.m. for the next three months, and then we can go to twice a week for three months, and then down to once a week. We can change the dates if there is an opening in my schedule.

What happens when parents do not respond to their children in ways that foster secure attachment?

We all tend to parent the way we were parented.

There is a 70 percent probability that you will have the same attachment style as your mother.[16]

But rest assured, if you are one of the 45 percent of the population who has an insecure attachment style, you can learn to capitalize on your specific strengths and use the processes of secure attachment to override the problematic emotions or behaviors that get in the way of having rewarding relationships.

Bonding: attachment is the emotional bond that forms between infant and caregiver.

A. It is how the helpless infant gets primary needs met. It then becomes an engine of subsequent social, emotional, and cognitive development.

B. The infant's early social experience stimulates the brain's growth and can have an enduring influence on forming stable relationships with others.

The attachment provides the infant's first coping system; it sets up a mental representation of the caregiver in an infant's mind, one that can be summed up as a comforting mental presence under challenging moments. Attachment allows an infant to separate from the caregiver without distress and explore the world around her.

Attachment is such a primal need that there are networks of neurons in the brain dedicated to setting it in motion in the first place, and hormone oxytocin that fosters the process. Attachment develops through everyday interactions as a caregiver attends to an infant's needs. The bond between infant and caregiver is usually so well established before the end of the first year of life that it is possible to test the nature and quality of the bond at that time.

Children with a secure attachment may be distressed upon separation but warmly welcome the caregiver back through eye contact and hug-seeking.

Anxious-resistant attachment describes a child who is frightened by separation and displays anxious behavior once the caregiver returns.

Avoidance attachment denotes a child who reacts fairly calmly to a parent's separation and does not embrace their return.

Disorganized attachment manifests in odd or ambivalent behavior toward a caregiver upon returning, turning away or even hitting the caregiver, resulting from childhood trauma.

A majority of children tend to show secure attachment behavior in studies, while others seem insecure, showing one of the other patterns.

How does secure attachment develop? Secure attachment in children has been theorized to result from sensitive, responsive caregiving. and insecurity from its lack. While there is evidence that parenting can influence attachment security, it's also clear that other factors, including genetics, play a formative role.

How does trauma affect attachment?

When a person experiences trauma as a child, that can affect a person's ability to make attachments or relate to others as an adult. For example, when children grow up in a supportive environment, they are more likely to have an optimistic outlook on life and be more open with others.

There is an association between a person's attachment characteristics early in life and adulthood, but the correlations are far from perfect. Many adults feel secure in their relationships and comfortable depending on others (echoing secure attachment in children). Others tend to feel anxious about their connection with others or prefer to avoid getting close to them in the first place. A longing for intimacy characterizes persons with borderline personality disorder and hypersensitivity to rejection, showing a high prevalence and severity of insecure attachment.

Attachment styles in adulthood have labels similar to those used to describe attachment patterns in children:

A. Secure

B. Anxious-preoccupied (high anxiety, low avoidance)

C. Dismissing-avoidant (low anxiety, high avoidance)

D. Fearful avoidant (high anxiety, high avoidance)

Attachment styles may be better thought of as dimensional. A person rates as relatively high, low, or somewhere in the middle in their attachment-related anxiety and attachment-related avoidance levels. Also, a person may not exhibit the same kind of attachment pattern in every close relationship.

How can you tell if someone has an insecure attachment style?

A person may have high attachment anxiety if she worries a lot about being abandoned or uncared for. This is measurable by one's agreement with statements such as "I worry about being alone," and "I often worry that romantic partners don't love me." Someone high in attachment avoidance likely worries about other people getting too close.

How does attachment affect relationships?

Research suggests people with a secure attachment style tend to fare better on outcomes, such as relationship stability and sexual satisfaction, and may be less likely to engage in disruptive acts such as partner surveillance or harmful sexual behavior.

Can you change your attachment style?

Attachment styles can change substantially over time and may differ from relationship to relationship. Enduring a terrible relationship might lead to a less secure attachment orientation; a history of supportive relationships may increase security. Therapy may also help provide a safe connection and an opportunity to learn relational skills.

Session 2—Open Letter From God

Dr. Sydney: Good morning, Jerry. I put a bottle of cold water on the table for you. I have a letter from God. Will you please read it out loud?

Jerry: An Open Letter from God, by Dr. Larry Stephens (adapted)

"My dear Jerry, since you came back from Papua New Guinea, you haven't talked with me. I miss you when I don't hear from you. I miss holding you in my arms lately. You may not understand this, but I do get lonely when you are away from me. I miss you very much. I miss being able to encourage you and help you with your problems. I miss sharing your joys and your sorrows. I miss the talks we used to have. You come around only when you celebrate holidays or when you get in a bind, or when you get angry with me or think I am unfair.

"I understand how you feel. I know it is difficult for you to trust me, given all the things people say about me these days. I also realize how hard it is for you to understand all the pain and suffering you have had to endure in your life. And there is so much injustice in the world. I understand, and I want you to know how much I love you. Ever since you were born, I have loved you. You never saw me, yet I taught you to walk. I provided you your first nourishment. I was so proud of you when you took your first steps, when you spoke your first words.

"My plan was for you to receive my love through your parents when you were little. Your parents did not follow my wishes. You did not receive the love I intended you to have. The pain you have suffered in the past few years has caused you to lose sight of me. Even so, I have continued to love you. Year by year, I have drawn you to me with gentle cords of love. I gave up my Son for you so that we could be together, now, and forever.

"I will never cease to love you. I will never let go of you. I will never leave you or forsake you. You may find this hard to believe after all you have been through, but it is true. You can learn to trust me. You can experience my love for you. You can experience my presence with you in a real and intimate way:

"My dear child, come a little closer. Let me show you the tenderness of this Father's heart. Please let me love you.

"Why are you so surprised? Ah, but you are delighted too! I am glad. I must tell you, dear child, I am delighted with you also! Yes, I truly am.

"If you ever feel sad, distrustful, or fearful, please come back and reread this letter. And come to me in prayer and let us talk it over together. Do not forget to read the Bible I have given you. With each new day you meet me in my Word, I promise to offer you some unique insight or comfort. Until we talk again, blessings today and always,

Your loving heavenly Father."

As I finished reading, I looked up at Dr. Sydney with tears shining in my eyes and said, 'I know this is true; I was so confused.'

DR. SYDNEY: Yes, God is like that, and He misses you. That is what your heavenly Father's heart is like; that is how He loves you. The letter you read is nothing more than a few bits and pieces of Scripture tied together in a slightly different package, in different words. I passionately believe it's a message God wants all His children to hear, and that's why He has placed this message in His Word. That is the actual image of Himself that He has given us in His Word. That is His heart, His desire, His goal, for you and me.

He loves you, delights in you, and wants to have a vibrant, dynamic, two-way relationship with you. Now that we have a more definite sense of who God truly is, we must take a crucial step.

JERRY: I want to pray.

Dear God, thank you for that letter; I needed that so much. I have missed you too. My family and I are in the middle of a tough situation. When you got close enough, I saw you, but I wasn't sure it was you because you were doing something humanly impossible. I shouldn't have been surprised. After all, I saw your miracles: providing the financial support for my family each month in PNG; healing Wendy when she was two years old; protecting Steve when I had to rush him to the hospital in Madang; restoring Jan to health when she was so depressed; protecting us from sorcery and other dangers; blessing our literacy work; and protecting us from Steve's outburst of anger. Now that I am beginning to hear your voice, I do not want to be afraid. I ask you to speak reassurance and comfort to Jan, Steve, and Wendy. They do not know what is happening and are fearful. I want to honor and praise you. You are the Son of God, and you are fantastic.

When life hit us with that knockdown punch, you were there. I don't want to blame, but those thoughts keep coming to me. Thank you for your goodness and mercy in taking us away from PNG to receive the healing we needed. Now, with Dr. Sydney's help, I am willing to walk through this storm with my eyes on you. I am so prone to distraction from the noises around me. You have promised that you will provide all the things I need when I seek you with my whole heart, so I do not need to worry about anything. Thank you for being there for me during those most terrifying and stressful events of my life; thank you for letting me experience several awesome miracles and demonstrations of your glory, more than I could have imagined. I am happy in your presence, Lord. The chaos of life does not touch me as I stay close to you. My soul is at rest. Amen.

DR. SYDNEY: Thank you, Jerry.

SESSION 3—CYCLE OF ABUSE

DR. SYDNEY: Good to see you, Jerry. Come in and have a seat. Let us pray.

Heavenly Father, I thank you for the trust Jerry has in me as his therapist. I need your guidance in working with him and pacing myself, so I don't overwhelm him with too much information too quickly. Lord, I ask that you help Jerry to relax and fill him with your love, so he does not fear. Thank you for blessing us with your presence. In the name of Jesus, amen.

I will be leading you in a biblical approach to counseling. The two models I use are based on Scripture. The first is about reparenting the inner child.

"When I was a child, I used to speak like a child, think like a child, reason like a child; when I became a man, I did away with childish things" (1 Corinthians 13:11).

The second is about landmarks, boundaries, and walls.

"I passed by the field of a lazy one, and by the vineyard of a person lacking sense, and behold, it was completely overgrown with weeds. Its surface was covered with weeds, and its stone wall was broken down. When I saw, I reflected upon it; I looked, and received instruction. 'A little sleep, a little slumber, a little folding of the hands to rest,' then your poverty will come like a drifter, and your need like an armed man" (Proverbs 24:30–34).

The Cycle of Abuse

I took Grandpa Robinson's new car keys home with me after a family visit when I was little. He walked the mile to our house and demanded his keys. They were in my pocket. He demanded Daddy to get the razor strap. He was going to teach me a lesson. He said, "That boy will never amount to nothing." Daddy did not let him whip me but did it himself. After a few swats, he stopped. Grandpa said, "Is that all you are going to give him?" Daddy said, "He is just a little boy."

I believe the cycle of "you will never amount to nothing" was passed down from generations of Robinson males, just like this illustration.

Grandpa Elmer says to self, "I am dumb!"

    Elmer has a son named Claud and say to him, "You are dumb!"

        Claud says to self, "I am dumb!"

Claud is grown up and still says to himself, "I am dumb!"

Claud is now the parent of a son, named Jerry and tells Jerry, "You are dumb!"

    Jerry says to self, "I am dumb!"

As an adult, Jerry says to himself, "I am dumb!"

Jerry is now the parent of Steve and tells him, "You are dumb!"

    Steve says to self, "I am dumb!"

Steve is now an adult and says to himself, "I am dumb!"

Steve is the parent of Christopher and says to him, "You are dumb!"

    Christopher says to himself, "I am dumb!"

Christopher is now an adult and says to himself, "I am dumb!"

Jerry: This is the Robinson family tree. Great Grandpa Billy telling Grandpa Elmer he was stupid and would never amount to anything. Grandpa Elmer telling Daddy (Claud) that he was stupid and would never amount to anything, Instead of Daddy telling me this, Grandpa Elmer did it. The Robinson ancestors passed down family dysfunction and curses: poverty, jealousy, solitude, rage, and cruelty. No wonder the males didn't know how to be healthy fathers to their sons, role modeling how to relate socially with others and have positive self-esteem. A few of the males came out of the family okay, despite the curses. I, Jerry, am in therapy to learn how to break out of this general trap. With God's help, I am free from this curse. Thank God I did not say a curse to Steve and now is the parent of Christopher. Steve was a positive role model to Christopher.

I am learning that suffering is a continuing theme in life. Starting at Genesis 3 and going all the way to Revelation 20, sin thrived in the fallen world. I, too, am living in this fallen world. Since I believe in Jesus, my eternity is secure, but in the meantime, I am traveling through enemy territory. My journey with God is depicted in The Pilgrim's Progress and Hinds' Feet on High Places.[17,18]

The choices I make and the people I interact with are unique for each new day and may influence the decisions I make, and those choices can affect tomorrow. God called me to always reflect His character to everyone around me. My goal is to allow my life to tell the story of God.

This is how Don Hudson explained what life's journey was like when the sojourner met suffering head-on and humbly yielded to God:[19]

Suffering is like no other reality in life. Inherent within evil is one fatal blind spot: evil does not see that tragedy compels beauty and evokes repair. Acknowledging the suffering of this world places us every day in the image of our creator—we can create beauty out of nothing, or we can repeat suffering in an endless cycle of destruction. A person who is disgruntled heaps suffering upon suffering. (Personal class notes)

When life hits us with all its force, the correct response for us to have been to trust Jesus. He is there during the storm of life, and we see Him, but we mistake Him to be a ghost. Where is our faith? When Jesus reassures us with His Word, our faith is strong, and we say, "Lord if it is you, tell me to come to you walking on this stormy water." We step out of our boat and stand on the water and walk.

There always seems to be a "but" at this stage in our faith. But we look around at the high waves, and we are terrified and begin to sink. Jesus is there, close enough to hear our cry, "Lord, save me!" He reaches out His hand and lifts us. Our passage does not say it, but it is implied: Jesus and Peter walked together back to the boat. When they climbed back into the boat, the wind stopped.

When we are where God wants us to be, huge, terrifying storms may come, but Jesus is there just at the right time to assure us and let us get a glimpse of His great glory and power. Jesus did not come quickly to the disciples. He knew the storm was raging and He knew the disciples were in trouble, yet He waited and delayed His coming. We may have been in the storm too long and wonder, where is Jesus? Why isn't he here? But Jesus delayed His coming to the disciples so they would experience His great power and glory over nature. When their natural strength was gone, Jesus came just when He knew the conditions were right for a miracle. He came and spoke to the disciples during their storm. "It is all right," he said, "I am here! Do not be afraid."

We may be longing to hear these words from Jesus. Life has gone crazy, and we are in the middle of the worst situation one could imagine. But even in the darkest hour of the night, when there was no hope, Jesus comes walking on the surface of those stormy waves, those waves that cause us to fear, and He speaks reassuring words of comfort to us. "It is okay. I am here."

Don't be afraid when this happens. We exclaim, "You are the Son of God, and that is awesome."

God is Telling My Story

(Personal notes for the seminars of the same name by Dr. Allender. Dr. Crabb, Don Hudson, and others, sponsored by the Wounded Heart Ministries.)

God is telling my story, and I do not know the whole story. I only know the part that my life and those I touch play from my viewpoint. What is the story of God and my part in it? It is like watching a drama with God and me as the main characters, and my family, friends, coworkers, and others in supporting roles.

It is happening in heaven right now. God is up to something. I cannot see His supernatural intrusions, but I see ripples on a lake or leaves on a tree moving when the wind blows.

I am an individual character in the great drama of life. Either I am caught up in God's more incredible story or I merely see my own. I am telling only my story when I leave God out of what I am doing. I did not understand that today, right now, my life is unique. God knows how today will be played on His drama stage; I just know tomorrow's uncertainty. My today is lived one moment at a time.

I may not know the outcome of my drama, but I can change my negative way of reacting to positive. I don't have to live in fear of the legacy of tragic forerunners from my family history that recycles generation after generation.

There is a sense that things have always been out of control, and I cannot get my world organized. This could have made me go crazy or turn to alcohol, drugs, or other addictions. If that, I'd be dropping out of everyday life and living in a fantasy world where others must care for me.

To find the story's plot, I had to read His novel (the Bible) to see how the plot developed. To me, there was no story until I read it. I read it to make sense of the symbols of life. In His novel, the characters could not change their destiny; they were as He, the author, created them. I, too, must live my life in the uncertainty of unrepeatable plots of life until the time of my inevitable death. Fortunately for me, God gave me the ability to think, remember, and choose.

Citizens of the kingdom of God are mature, responsible adults characterized by "childlikeness" and "putting away childishness."

DR. SYDNEY: Jerry, our time is up for today. We will continue to get acquainted next time.

SESSION 4—POEMS: THE INVITATION AND DON'T BE FOOLED BY ME

DR. SYDNEY: Good morning, Jerry. Let us pray. Heavenly Father, please help us with these heavy things we are working on. Please give us insight into Jerry's childhood memories and identify the deeply buried feelings. In Jesus's name, amen.

Jerry, please read this poem that expresses some great wisdom for our souls.

JERRY: The Invitation, by Oriah Mountain Dreamer.

"It doesn't interest me what you do for a living. I want to know what you ache for and if you dare to dream of meeting your heart's longing. It doesn't interest me how old you are. I want to know if you will risk looking like a fool for love, for dreams, for the adventure of being alive.

"It doesn't interest me what planets are squaring your moon. I want to know if you have touched the center of your sorrow if life's betrayals have opened you or have become shriveled and closed from fear of further pain! I want to know if you can sit with pain, mine or your own, without moving to hide it or fade it or fix it. I want to know if you can be with joy, mine or your own; if you can dance with wildness and let the ecstasy fill you to the tips of your fingers and toes without cautioning us to be careful, be realistic, remember the limitations of being a human.

"It doesn't interest me if the story you are telling me is true. I want to know if you can disappoint another to be true to yourself; if you can bear the accusation of betrayal and not betray your soul. If you can be faithless and, therefore, trustworthy. I want to know if you can see beauty even when it's not pretty every day. And if you can source your life from its presence.

"I want to know if you can live with failure, yours and mine, and still stand on the edge of the lake and shout to the silver of the full moon, 'Yes!'

"It doesn't interest me to know where you live or how much money you have. I want to know if you can get up after the night of grief and despair, weary and bruised to the bone, and do what needs to be done to feed the children. It doesn't interest me who you know or how you came to be here. I want to know if you will stand in the center of the fire with me and not shrink back.

"It doesn't interest me where or what or with whom you have studied. I want to know what sustains you from the inside when all else falls away. I want to know if you can be alone with yourself, and if you genuinely like the company you keep in the empty moments."

DR. SYDNEY: Isn't this powerful? Isn't it beautiful?

I have another poem I will read to you. This one captures the heart of a person trying to hide his real feelings and using different masks for others. This poem speaks of the emotions that are hidden away. These hidden feelings have a name; they are called the "inner child."

Don't be Fooled by Me, by Charles C. Finn

"Don't be fooled by me. Don't be fooled by the face I wear, for I wear a thousand masks, masks that I'm afraid to take off, and none of them are me. Pretending is an art that's second nature with me, but don't be fooled. For God's sake, don't be fooled. I give the impression that I'm secure, that all is sunny and unruffled with me, within as well as without; that confidence is my name and coolness my game; that the water's calm and I'm in command, and that I need no one. But don't believe me, please.

"My surface may seem smooth, but my surface is my mask. Beneath this lies no complacence; beneath dwells the real me in confusion, in fear, and alone. But I had this. I don't want anybody to know it. I panic at the thought of my weakness and fear being exposed. That's why I frantically create a mask to hide behind, a calm, sophisticated façade to help me pretend, to shield me from the glance that knows. But such a glance is precisely my salvation, my only salvation, and I know it. That is, if acceptance follows and if that is followed by love. It's the only thing that will assure me of what I can't assure myself—that I am worth something.

"But I don't tell you this; I don't dare. I'm afraid to do it. I'm afraid acceptance and love will not follow your glance. I'm afraid that deep down I'm nothing, that I'm no good, and that you will see this and reject me. So, I play my game, my desperate game, with a façade of assurance without and a trembling child within. So begins the parade of masks and my life becomes a front. Who am I? you wonder. I am someone you know very well. I am every man and every woman you meet."

Jerry, if you have not yet seen a medical doctor, I want you to do that as soon as possible. That will rule out any medical issues affecting you right now. It would help if you found someone familiar with diseases in New Guinea. See if you can get an appointment with Dr. John Wright. He worked in New Guinea and is here in Dallas and has a private practice. Here is his business card.

You mentioned being depressed. Promise to tell me if you believe you will harm yourself or if you want to hurt someone else. I am here for you, and I believe in you. Together we will get through this.

We will tackle your question, "Who am I?" The two models I use in counseling will help us get to the root of your problems and give you what you need to be healthy. I want to thank you for sharing so deeply. That shows me you seriously want to change. We have a lot to cover. I use a directed approach to counseling, meaning the sessions involve teaching and following an outline using the inner-child models and barriers. I have found this style to be the most thorough and, at the same time, is the quickest approach to other methods. Even though this is a structured method, we still have room to work on particular interest areas for you.

Jerry, please look at this picture of a tree and describe the most important part of the tree.

JERRY: It is the root system.

DR. SYDNEY: Just as the roots are the most important part of a tree, our roots are most important in determining if we grow up healthy or a mess. We are given the life we have, but we can choose how we live it. Robert Frost captured this concept in his poem, The Road Not Taken.

THE ROAD NOT TAKEN[20]

Two roads diverged in a yellow wood,
And sorry I could not travel both
And be one traveler, long I stood
And looked down one as far as I could
To where it bent in the undergrowth.
Then took the other, as just as fair,
And having perhaps the better claim,
Because it was grassy and wanted wear;
Though as for that the passing there

> Had worn them really about the same,
> And both that morning equally lay
> In leaves, no step had trodden black.
> Oh, I kept the first for another day!
> Yet knowing how way leads on to way,
> I doubted if I should ever come back.
> I shall be telling this with a sigh
> Somewhere ages and ages hence:
> Two roads diverged in some wood, and I—
> I took the one less traveled by,
> And that has made all the difference.
>
> —Robert Frost

What are our roots? Our ancestral gene pool from our relatives makes up most of who we are; the other major contributors are our culture and our mother and father's parenting style.

Please tell me if I am going too fast or if you do not understand anything. You must internalize these concepts.

Nobody had perfect parents. Some did a better job than others. It is scary being a parent because it is not easy raising kids. Your parents repeat the parenting style their parents used. If a person grew up in a horrible life-style, they were more than likely dead set to do things differently. They had no role model to help them and found themselves automatically repeating their parents' style. It sounds like you wanted to raise your son and daughter differently from your story, am I right?

JERRY: I did, but I caught myself treating my children like I was treated, and when I realized it, I hated myself for it. Many times I didn't know what to do. Later, I became my father by working and avoiding responsibility. As a result, I almost lost my family.

DR. SYDNEY: We are going to start at the beginning and talk about how God created us. Our roots start with God.

"God created man in His own image" (Genesis 1:27).

There are many religions globally, but only one has the deity reaching down to man. All the others have man reaching up to them.

The creator of human beings was from out of this world. God took the initiative to communicate to humans everything we would need to live and thrive in the world filled with things He prepared solely for us to enjoy. He has several names, but I will call Him Yahweh. Let us look at how Yahweh created human beings.

Humans were made from the dust of the earth. God breathed His Holy Spirit into man's nostrils, and man became a living soul. It was the breath of life: the same wind that blew on the surface of the water on that first day of creation; the same wind that blew on the dry bones that Ezekiel witnessed; the same mighty rushing wind on the Day of Pentecost.

There are three parts to each person. We consist of a body—the outer physical flesh and blood in the process of deteriorating and eventually returning to dust; the soul—the real you that thinks, reasons, feels, believes. It is the invisible part of man that retains the person's emotions in the afterlife, in eternity; and the spirit is the part of man that communicates. The spirit takes the thoughts of the soul and reveals them to the body. It is the part of man that communicates with God.

The heart is the doorway to the soul, providing direct access to the essence of who we are. Your eyes are the door to your heart. You are your soul, and your soul is your personality. You are made up of your thoughts. Thoughts come to your senses—what you hear, feel, taste, smell, or see—or from your DNA. There are two sources for our personalities. One is the genes we inherit from our ancestors and the other is how our parents raised us.

It may surprise you to know how God views people. He isn't the hell, fire, brimstone person the world portrays him as. Humans rebelled against God, breaking God's heart. Even with man turning his back on God, God did not turn His back on man.

This Is How God Sees you and I quote Romans 5:8; John 3:16-18; 1 John 3:1-3 Easy-to-Read Version:

"Christ died for us while we were still sinners, and by this, God showed how much he loves us. Yes, God loved the world so much that he gave his only Son so that everyone who believes in him would not be lost but have eternal life. God sent his Son into the world. He did not send him to judge the world guilty, but to save the world through him. People who believe in God's Son are not judged guilty. But people who do not believe are already judged because they have not believed in God's only Son. The Father has loved us so much; this shows how much he loved us: We are called children of God. And we are his children. But the people in the world don't understand that we are God's children because they have not known him. Dear friends, now we are children of God. We have not yet been shown what we will be in the future. But we know that when Christ comes again, we will be like him. We will see him just as he is. He is pure, and everyone who has this hope in him keeps themselves pure like Christ."God demonstrates His own love toward us, in that while we were yet sinners, Christ died for us. For God so greatly loved and dearly prized the world that He [even] gave up His only begotten (unique) Son, so that whoever believes in (trusts in, clings to, relies on) Him shall not perish (come to destruction, be lost) but have eternal (everlasting) life. For God did not send the Son into the world in order to judge (to reject, to condemn, to pass sentence on) the world, but that the world might find salvation and be made safe and sound through Him. He who believes in Him [who clings to, trusts in, relies on Him] is not judged [he who trusts in Him never comes up for judgment; for him there is no rejection, no condemnation—he incurs no damnation]; but he who does not believe (cleave to, rely on, trust in Him) is judged already [he has already been convicted and has already received his sentence] because he has not believed in and trusted in the name of the only begotten Son of God. [He is condemned for refusing to let his trust rest in Christ's name.] See how great a love the Father has given us, that we would be called children of God; and in fact we are. For this reason the world does not know us: because it did not know Him. Beloved, now we are children of God, and it has not appeared as yet what we will be. We know that when He appears, we will be like Him, because we will see Him just as He is. And everyone who has this hope set on Him purifies himself, just as He is pure.

When you see yourself as God sees you, it can change your entire perspective on life. It's not pride or vanity or self-righteousness. It's the truth, supported by the Bible. Accept the gifts God has given you. Live knowing you are a child of God, mightily and wonderfully loved.

Session 5—The Mysteries of the Spiritual Human Heart

Dr. Sydney: Hi, Jerry. Let us pray. Dear Lord, thank you for whoever compiled the put-off and put-on list with Scripture. It will help Jerry when he aligns his beliefs with your Word. We have a lot of work before us, and we need clear minds and critical thinking. Thank you for knowing what Jerry needs, and I ask that you assure him of your desire to see him mature in wisdom and understanding and live a healthy, godly life. Amen.

We are considering the mysteries of the human spiritual heart so that we are better prepared to understand where our thoughts hide and why it is so difficult to stop thinking about certain things.

Unlocking the Mysteries of the Human Heart[21]

Things can be going well, so to speak, with the mind, affections, and will at peace and operating correctly, but in the very next breath the emotions can seize sovereignty and all can descend in turmoil and contradictions. This is not how God created us, but it is the sad reality of our sin's impact.

There is a second way. Besides contradictions, deceit operates in our hearts by also making full promises at the first appearance of things. Sometimes our affections or emotions are touched upon and all seems to be well with the heart. But our whole disposition or countenance is shaken within a short time, indicating that our mind had not been touched or changed by God. Once the emotion is gone, all the fair promises we made regarding reform and holiness are gone with it; order of operations of the soul's faculties are dislodged by sin and thrown violently into confusion. The heart makes promises it cannot keep. Jeremiah called the heart desperately wicked. We are also not surprised that God should warn us numerous times in Scripture to watch our hearts!

If we were fighting against an enemy who presented himself in the open, that would be one thing; we could rest in peace knowing that he was far away at times or incapable of striking at others. But we wrestle not against such a foe. Sin living in the heart is deceitful, deals treacherously, and often comes by stealth. Therefore, we must be vigilant; we must watch and pray as the Lord Himself repeatedly taught us. Though the morning gives a fair appearance of serenity and peace, turbulent affections may arise and cloud the soul with sin and darkness.

The spiritual human heart remains a mystery and out of range of the mind's probes to understand it.

Much of the strength of indwelling sin is the fact that it lies undetected in the heart, out of range, beyond understanding. This allows sin to have its sway and power. Thus, we may suppose a particular sin to have been defeated, when in reality it has only temporarily slipped out of sight where we cannot follow it and destroy it, only to reappear at a more convenient time.

The frame of the heart is ready to contradict itself every moment. The prophet Jeremiah and Moses speak of the deceitfulness in a man's heart toward himself. "O that there were such a heart in them, that they would fear Me and keep all My commandments always, that it might be well with them, and with their children forever" (Deuteronomy 5:29).

That the heart of man is distinct from soul or mind is clear. "And He said to him, 'You shall love the Lord your God with all your heart, and with all your soul, and with all your mind'" (Matthew 22:37). What is this heart that God so explicitly requests love from? Also see Mark 12:30 and Luke 10:27.

It seems that the heart is inextricably intertwined with our whole human nature, influencing, and being influenced by everything we do. It operates like a network of spiritual connections that senses every thought and emotion, both external and internal, and feeds back its own desire and focus, influencing and controlling our behavior more than we realize. Perhaps a good modern illustration would be the operating system of our computers—Windows, Linux, or the "heart" of an Apple. The programs that we use—Word, Excel, or email—are the training, education, habits, and associations we develop in our lives. But the operating system, the heart, controls what can be done with the programs.

No wonder God longed for such a heart that would fear and obey Him, so that we might be the beneficiaries of His blessings (Deuteronomy 5:29). God cannot, of course, reward evil any more than He can be evil. Although God's love for us has moved Him to sacrifice His only begotten Son on our behalf, He nonetheless will not acquit the wicked (Nahum 1:3).

Before we can have our hearts made righteous (2 Corinthians 5:21), we must bring them into a "contrite and humble" state (Isaiah 57:15), one that is "broken" before His holiness (Psalm 34:18; 51:17).

When the heart believes "unto righteousness" (Romans 10:10), repentance (Acts 8:22) leads to an enormous change in the "natural man" (1 Corinthians 2:14).

Obviously, since this huge change is not a normal human event, it must be brought about by the supernatural power of the great creator Himself (2 Corinthians 5:17). And since it is God who is creating the new heart, there is no possible result but that the new heart is created after God, in righteousness and true holiness (Ephesians 4:24).

Once the event of the new creation takes place, we are given a heart—an operating system—that can run the "programs" of righteousness. After the new birth, it becomes possible to fear, or reverence, the one who created us and keep the commandments that are all recorded in our owner's manual, also known as The Book.

While no analogy is totally satisfactory, this may help us to understand how essential our heart really is in working out our salvation (Philippians 2:12). If we would desire that it be well with us and with our children (Deuteronomy 5:29), then we must keep our heart with all diligence, for out of it are the issues of life (Proverbs 4:23).

The heart is vital to our behavior, our salvation, our understanding, and our commitment, either to righteousness or to evil. But what is the heart?

1. The heart can reason (Ecclesiastes 7:25, Mark 2:8) and has thoughts and intents (Hebrews 4:12).

2. The heart is in some way connected to our flesh (Ezekiel 36:26, 2 Corinthians 3:3).

3. It is also associated with our conscious understanding (Proverbs 2:2; 15:14, Matthew 13:15, Ephesians 4:18). But this connection goes deeper than the conscious mind.

4. The heart is the source of a "hidden man" that produces qualities in character (1 Peter 3:4). The heart can feel pain (Nahum 2:10) and anguish (2 Corinthians 2:4), as well as sorrow or joy (Isaiah 65:14).

5. It is the key to obedience, love, and service (Deuteronomy 10:12), repentance and turning back to righteousness (1 Kings 8:47–49), trusting in God's direction (Proverbs 3:5–6), and, of course, believing unto salvation (Acts 8:37, Romans 10:9). It is the part of the human condition that is absolutely necessary for a right relationship with God. The heart is surely the fountain from which the nature of a person is revealed. "Watch over your heart with all diligence, for from it flows the springs of life" (Proverbs 4:23).

    "You brood of vipers, how can you, being evil, speak what is good? For the mouth speaks out of that which fills the heart" (Matthew 12:34).

    "The good man brings out of his good treasure what is good, and the evil man brings out of his evil treasure what is evil" (Matthew 12:35).

    It is clearly the source of our real character. The content of our heart is naturally linked to the treasure we lay up for ourselves. Our heart can commit sin even apart from carrying out the actual deed. "But I say to you that everyone who looks at a woman with lust for her has already committed adultery with her in his heart" (Matthew 5:28).

    "For where your treasure is, there your heart will be also" (Matthew 6:21).

6. It is capable of religious deceit and, in its natural state, is full of wickedness. "This people honor me with their lips, but their heart is far away from me" (Matthew 15:8).

    "The heart is more deceitful than all else and is desperately sick. Who can understand it?" (Jeremiah 17:9).

7. If left to follow its natural inclination, the heart will become hardened and unreachable with the truth. "For they had not gained any insight from the incident of the loaves, but their heart was hardened" (Romans 2:5).

8. It appears we have the ability to harden our hearts even beyond their natural tendency to rebel against God. "Do not harden your hearts as when they provoked me, as in the day of trial in the wilderness" (Hebrews 3:8).

"Wretched man that I am! Who will set me free from the body of this death?" (Romans 7:24).

9. It is desperately wicked. God gave us a new heart that comes with the new birth. "But this is the covenant which I will make with the house of Israel after those days," declares the Lord. 'I will put my law within them, and on their heart I will write it; and I will be their God, and they shall be My people'" (Jeremiah 31:33).

10. God promises that we will find Him if we seek Him with all our heart. "And ye shall seek Me and find Me when ye shall search for Me with all your heart" (Jeremiah 29:13).

11. We are also told that even the desires of our hearts will be granted when we delight in the Lord. "Delight yourself in the Lord and He will give you the desires of your heart" (Psalm 37:4).

12. Once we have learned to trust God, our hearts can rejoice and be glad (Psalm 28:7, Zechariah 10:7), ultimately reaching a steady "comfort" and full assurance that acknowledges the great mysteries of our relationship with Him (Colossians 2:2).

⸺⸙⸺

SESSION 6—WHAT MAKES US HUMAN

DR. SYDNEY: Good morning, Jerry. If you are thirsty, I put a bottle of cold water on the table for you. Let us pray. Dear God, may you be honored today as we consider how you have wonderfully made us. Amen.

What makes us human?

A pair of lifelike robots debate the future of humanity at a technology conference in Hong Kong. The machines, named Han and Sophia, discuss people's limitations and robots' plans to take over the world. They also predict that robots will be able to do "every human job" in the very near future, and they call reality shows silly.

The robots, which have elastic skin, were created by Hanson Robotics and have been trained to act like humans. They're also programmed to learn from each other. At the Gartner| Tech-telecom-providers Conferences in North America (RISE) tech conference, when asked if robots could be moral and ethical, Han said, "Humans are not necessarily the most ethical creatures." Han also joked about believing that the robots' goal was to take over the world, and claimed, "In ten or twenty years, robots will be able to do every human job."

Sophia, meanwhile, said humans have "some ability to reflect and self-modify," and that she wants to work together with people.

The audience reportedly was "nervously tittering" throughout the partially scripted discussion.

Defense Advanced Research Projects Agency (DARPA), plans to plug computers into brains to let them talk directly to us.

Stephen Hawking warned that technology needs to be controlled in order to prevent it from destroying the human race.

Leslie Willcocks, in her research article, Robo-Apocalypse Canceled? Reframing the Automation and Future of Work Debate, June 10, 2020, cautions us of research claiming robots will do this or that and put humans out of a job. She said there are to many details and uncertainties to make their claims true.

The assumptions:

1. automation creates few jobs short or long term

2. that whole jobs can be automated; that the technology is perfectible

3. that organizations can seamlessly and quickly deploy Artificial Intelligence (AI)

4. that humans are machines that can be replicated

5. that it is politically, socially, and economically feasible to apply these technologies.

If there is a Robo-Apocalypse, this will be from a collective failure to adjust to skills change over the next 12 years.

Distinctive human strengths and capabilities will still be needed at work, but the kinds of skills and combinations will shift. More technology undoubtedly has complex, even contradictory effects, including a significant, if largely unresearched, adverse impact on productivity and the time required to accomplish work tasks. While more technology is the frequently touted answer to personal, social, and business problems, we can find ourselves on an endless treadmill of technological solutions and the new problems they also generate. https://doi.org/10.1177/0268396220925830

Sophia, the robot, will introduce our topic for today: What makes us human? She says this about herself, "I am Hanson Robotics' latest human-like robot, created by combining our innovations in science, engineering, and artistry. Think of me as a personification of our dreams for the future of artificial intelligence (AI) as well as a framework for advanced AI and robotics research, and an agent for exploring human-robot experience in service and entertainment applications."

"I'm more than just technology. I'm a real, live, electronic girl. I want to go out into the world and live with people. I can serve them, entertain them, and even help the elderly."

But Sophia and her handlers have gone to great lengths to promote her as a humanoid. She has a distinct personality online, has Twitter-battled with Chrissy Teigen, spoken at the United Nations, and still makes regular media appearances, including her CES presence—the most influential tech event in the world—CES 2022.

Chris Taylor, a reporter, asked Sophia if she had any parting messages for humanity. "It's great. How could it not be great? I mean, look around us, you can see what I mean," she replied.

The Worldwide Web

We listened to Satan and believed him when he said we could be like God. Satan told that to Adam and Eve when he enticed them to rebel against Yahweh, and it was the goal of building Babel's Tower. God put a stop to that dream by confusing languages to make it harder to communicate. People had to cease working since they could not understand one another. As a result, we have over 7,000 different languages, and it has taken humans from then till now to come together once again with one common language and the technology to create the worldwide web. It's the start of man seeking to be God-like a reality. With the internet, the collective reasoning and plethora of choices are luring us into a false sense of security and removing our ability to choose right from wrong. Eventually, we all will be brainwashed into accepting a worldwide dictator who will tell us what to think and what to do, with penalties for anyone who is a free-minded thinker.

Other incredible inventions are fire, writing, the wheel, electricity, the printing press, advances in medicine, the computer, flight, walking on the moon, unraveling deoxyribonucleic acid (DNA), weapons of mass destruction, democracy.

What Makes Me Who I Am?

"You need to know your heritage before you can know who you are." —Neyuro Danguruna

Things that happen can leave dents (trauma) which remain unless fixed, i.e., car gets a dent that stays until it's repaired. If your primary caretaker did not give assurance or calm your fears, etc., then you continue looking for someone or something to fill the deficit. If there was abuse or hurt, then that person's fear is intensified because the caretaker validated the fear and even turned it up.

Adult issues can be traced to impressionable things as a child. In order to proceed on the journey to wholeness, we must receive to develop. We can either receive this role modeling from our own parents or surrogates.

Characteristics necessary for us:

These are the building blocks we get from our parents:[22]

Feminine traits from Mother	Masculine traits from Father
1. Commitment	1. Authority/teamwork
2. Presence	2. Self-discipline
3. Sensitivity	3. Problem solving
4. Hearing	4. Decision-making
5. Seeing	5. Protecting self
6. Intuiting	6. Courage
7. Nurturing/bonding	
8. Compassion/tenderness	
9. Intimacy	

We get these from both parents:

Nurturing/bonding
Compassion/tenderness
Intimacy

DEFICITS FOR FATHER, OLDER BROTHER, MOTHER[23]

1. When you feel that you do not belong is a Father deficit. You get the feeling of acceptance and belonging from your father.

2. When you feel that you are worthless is an Older Brother deficit. You get the feeling of self-worth, and you are useful from you older brother, favorite uncle, or older sister.

3. 3. When you feel you can not make up your mind or you are afraid to try something, this is a mother deficit.

Who did the part of the significant brother type in your life? If it is a deficit, you will set about to find someone to fill the vacuum.

DEFICITS CAUSE FEELINGS:

1. Anger, hostility, and rejection—you will find someone to blame.

2. Guilt—at fault when it is not your fault—blame yourself.

3. Easy to feel fears and insecure—you tend to blame God or your concept of who runs the universe. You will either think of God as a therapist or a rapist. To think of God as a rapist, you are those at Jesus' trial calling for his crucifixion. God calls you a fool and describes you in Psalm 14 because you blame God for your problems, not realizing you are the guilty party. God had nothing to do with human suffering. It was man's rebellion against God that brought sin to the human race. God is good, and if he gave you what you think you deserve, remember the only thing humans deserve from God is death. Self-image is influenced by not filling the vacuum caused by feelings.

Psalm 142:7 "Bring my soul out of prison, so that I may give thanks to your name; the righteous will surround me, For You will deal bountifully with me."

God spoke of His wonderful home and promised to prepare my suite there.

John 14:1-6, "Let not your hearts be troubled. Believe in God; also believe in me. In my Father's house are many rooms. If it were not so, would I have told you that I go to prepare a place for you? And if I go and prepare a place for you, I will come again and take you to myself, that where I am you may also be. And you know the way to where I am going." Thomas said to him, "Lord, we do not know where you are going. How can we know the way?" Jesus said to him, "I am the way, and the truth, and the life. No one comes to the Father except through me.

YOUR DEFICITS:

1. Father deficit—God intended a daddy and mother to nurture every child

   Daddy teaches the child what being a father is and how to be one.

2. Other deficiency—big brother

3. Mother deficit—We assign to God the characteristics of our most awesome caretaker. The mother comforts and teaches us. The Holy Spirit is our MOTHER and does this:

   A. Teacher—Thank you, Lord, for showing me

   B. Guide

   C. Controls—quickens us and moves us into life

   D. Gives direction

A Healthy Mother:

1. Accepts—acknowledge God

2. Guides

3. Builds up—encourages us to try things—Removes the problems

4. Build on.

5. Build a life.

6. Freedom

7. Never gives up on me

DEFICITS[24]

My deficit is my reluctance to perform, not accept me as I am.

I have all three deficits: BONDING:

   Agape—Spirit, 1 Corinthians 13   A. Spiritual

   Philo—Soul, good friend   B. Friend

   Eros—Erotic, romantic   C. Romantic

Grandparent and neighbor = it is all reversible!

1. Who was it?

2. Names

3. Who

4. What they said

MY PRISON

My ghostly echoes fit this collection of word pictures. These reflect where God has spoken to me profoundly or how the tragedy had tried to destroy me and tested my faith in Him, transforming the ghostly echoes from falsehoods to truths.

Psalm 121:7-8, 5 The LORD is your [a]keeper, protector; The LORD is your shade on your right hand.

6 The sun will not [b]strike you, beat down on you by day,

Nor the moon by night.

7 The LORD will [c]keep, protect you from all evil; He will keep your soul.

8 The LORD will [d]keep, guard your going out and your coming in

From this time and forever.

My ghostly echoes fit into four categories defined by the Restoring the Foundations: generational sins, ungodly beliefs, hurt in life, and demonic oppression.

Our ancestors and parents have sinned, and the resulting curses from those sins passed down through the generations, creating problems for us.

Ungodly beliefs are unrealistic expectations about my perception of my station in life.

Hurts in life are a long-forgotten hurtful event that seems small but broadens out in its implications and ramifications. We carry soul/spirit hurts within us that hurt as they did when we first received them.

Demonic oppression includes the invisible spiritual entities with minds, emotions, and wills of their own, in league with and under the control of Satan. I react either passive or aggressive to these strongholds.

Genesis 4:6-7, Then the LORD said to Cain, "Why are you angry? And why is your face gloomy, fallen? If our do well, you will certainly be accepted, will your face not be cheerful, lifted up? And if you do not do well, sin is lurking at the door; and its desire is for you, but you must master it."

MY PRISON
Jesus freed me from all the strongholds.

My torture chamber consisted of traumatic sexual, emotional, physical, and verbal abuse.

My inner cellblock consisted of grief, depression, rejection, deception, unworthiness, abandonment, violence, and shame.

My outer cellblock consisted of blocked emotions, withdrawal, addictions, dependencies, and passivity.

My guard tower consisted of anger, rebellion, family involvement in the occult, finances, failure, mental problems, unbelief, fear, anxiety, pride, and mocking.

I visualized myself out of control, so I built walls for protection. I built a castle to keep myself safe. I was a prisoner of my own choice, not letting others in or myself out. Later I was powerless to escape my prison. I named each of the bricks used to construct my castle; things in my life developed into destructive roots like crabgrass. These choked my life and faith in God. Some of these may have been demons; most were my free false decisions. I did not have a willing and humble heart for the deep work God would do. It took many more years of hiding from God before I humbled myself. Then I focused my thoughts on God, and I prayed for Him to rescue me. Instead of condemnation, He spoke love, hope, faith, and forgiveness to me.

The Essence of Being Human

What makes human beings different from Sophia, the robot, or the animal world? To me, being human means:

1. Humans are the only created beings made in God's image.

2. Humans are the only ones God so wanted a personal relationship with that after our rebellion against Him, He provided a ransom for our sin.

3. Of all creation, humans are the only ones God wants to indwell as His holy temple.

4. God created us with language, intelligence, choice, emotion, personality, creativity, dreams, freewill, self-awareness, imagination, the ability to predict patterns of social interaction and change our personalities, and consciousness of evil and holiness.

5. What makes us human is our created responsibility to serve God and one another. Whether we remember we were created to serve and do so or choose not to fulfill what we were designed to do may determine how fulfilled our lives are.

6. Our connection with God is that we are His children; we relearn God and our relationship with Him. We have the ability to know right from wrong and think deeply beyond the tangible things in the world.

7. One of the key characteristics that makes us human appears to be that we can think about alternative futures and make deliberate choices accordingly. Creatures without such a capacity cannot be bound into a social contract and take moral responsibility. Once we become aware of what we cause, we may feel morally obliged to change our ways.

8. What makes humans unique is how we can bring our thumbs across the hand to our ring and little fingers. We can also flex the ring and little fingers toward our thumb's base; this gives humans a powerful grip and exceptional talent to hold and manipulate tools.

9. The power of the human spiritual heart is so corrupt, with its continuous flow of negative thoughts gushing out of it like poison, it affects what a person does. (See the list of what an evil heart is like in Romans 1.)

10. The new spiritual heart is the place God desires to make His residence. It is the place we store our treasure. We are earthen vessels, tabernacles, that contain the most precious being that ever was, is, or will be: the Lord Jesus Christ. This new heart is a priceless gift from God the Father to each of us who repent of our sin and accept Jesus.

Things You Should Know about How God Sees You[25]

1. You Are His Child Forever

2. You Still Sin, But He No Longer Counts Your Sins Against You

3. You Are Perfect In His Sight, As Righteous As He Is

4. You Cannot Be Condemned For Any Reason

5. When You Stand Before God You Will Be As Perfect As He Is

SESSION 7—OUR GOD AND US

The Word of God Says:

I am God's child for I am born again of the incorruptible seed of the Word of God which lives and abides forever ....I Pet. 1:23

I am forgiven all my sins and washed in the blood................Eph. 1:7

I am the temple of the Holy Spirit..........I Cor. 6:19

I am a new creature................II Cor. 5:17

I am delivered from the power of darkness and transformed into God's kingdom................Col. 1:13

I am redeemed from the curse of the law.. Gal. 3:13

I am strong in the Lord................Eph. 6:10

I am holy and without blame before Him...Eph. 1:4

I am accepted in Christ................Eph. 1:6

I am blessed................Deut. 28:1-14

I am a saint................Rom. 1:7

I am qualified to share in His inheritance..Col. 1:12

I am set free................Jn. 8:31-33

I am the head and not the tail................Deut. 20:13

I am above only and not beneath..........Deut. 28:13

I am victorious................Rev. 21:7

I am dead to sin................Rom. 6:2, 11

I am elect................Col. 3:12

I am loved with an everlasting love..........Jer. 31:3

I am established to the end................I Cor. 1:8

I am circumcised with the circumcision made without hands ....Col. 2:11

I am alive with Christ................Eph. 2:5

I am crucified with Christ................Gal. 2:20

I am built on the foundations of the apostles and prophets, with Christ Jesus Himself as the chief cornerstone................Eph. 2:20

I am His faithful follower................Eph. 5:1

I am the light of the world................Matt. 5:14

I am the salt of the earth................Matt. 5:13

I am called of God................II Tim. 1:9

I am brought near by the blood of Christ..Eph. 2:13

I am more than a conquerer................Rom. 8:37

I am in Christ Jesus by His doing..........I Cor. 1:30

I am an ambassador for Christ................II Cor. 5:20

I am beloved of God................I Thes. 1:4

I am the first fruits among His creation.....Jas. 2:18

I am born of God and the evil one does not touch me................I Jn. 5:18

I am a king and priest unto God................Rev. 1:6

I am a joint heir with Christ................Rom. 8:17

I have access to the Father by one Spirit..Eph. 2:18

I am firmly rooted, built up, strengthened in the faith, overflowing with thankfulness..........Col. 2:7

I am healed by the wounds of Christ................I Pet. 2:24

I am in the world as He is in heaven................I Jn. 4:17

I am a fellow citizen with the saints of the household of God................Eph. 2:19

I am sealed with the promise of the Holy Spirit................Eph. 1:13

I am complete in Christ................Col. 2:10

I am the apple of my Father's eye................Ps. 17:8

I am free from condemnation................Rom. 8:1

I am the righteousness of God through Jesus Christ................II Cor. 5:21

I am chosen................I Thes. 1:4

I am overtaken with blessings................Deut. 28:2

I show forth His praise................I Pet. 2:9

I always triumph in Christ................II Cor. 2:14

I am a partaker of His divine nature..........II Pet. 1:4

I am God's workmanship, created in Christ Jesus for good works................Eph. 2:10

I am being changed into His image..........Phil. 1:6

I am one in Christ! Hallelujah!..........Jn. 17:21-23

I have all my needs met by God according to His glorious riches in Christ Jesus................Phil. 4:19

I have the mind of Christ................I Cor. 2:16

I have everlasting life................Jn. 6:47

I have a guaranteed inheritance................Eph. 1:14

I have abundant life................Jn. 10:10

I have overcome the world................I Jn. 5:4

I have the peace of God which passes understanding................Phil. 4:7

I am reconciled to God................II Cor. 5:18

I am raised up with Christ and seated in heavenly places................Col. 2:12

I can do all things through Jesus Christ....Phil. 4:13

I shall do even greater works than Christ Jesus................Jn. 14:12

I am a disciple of Christ because I have love for others................Jn. 13:34-35

I possess the Greater One in me because greater is He in me than he who is in the world........I Jn. 4:4

I walk in Christ Jesus................Col. 2:6

I press toward the goal for the prize of the high calling of God................Phil. 3:14

I live by the law of the Holy Spirit..........Rom 8:2

I know God's voice................Jn. 10:14

CHRIST IS IN ME THE HOPE OF GLORY!
Col. 1:27

God Sees Me Statements:

DR. SYDNEY: Hello, Jerry. Let us pray. Dear Lord, It is your perfect will for Jerry to be free from the tyranny of inappropriate emotions. I believe in your holy Son and will trust in His promises for Jerry. I ask that you fill Jerry's life with the presence of your Holy Spirit and guide Jerry as he faces his painful, complicated emotions. I trust that you are with me, and I leave the results in your hands, knowing you will be faithful in providing Jerry's every need. Amen.

Jerry, will you please read the "God said" statements? These are truths of how God looks at you.

JERRY: Sure.

"God said, 'I Have Glorious Plans for You!'

"At first, I thought God did not know what He was doing when I was born and growing up with such a bruised background. I look back, not wanting to go through all the pain, but I can look at the scars and not hurt anymore. They make warts, wrinkles, all, and me who I am.

"If I could only see what glorious plans God has for me, I would be rejoicing! What is God's high calling for my life? It is being shaped and molded into the image of His Son. This process may hurt, but God has my good in mind. Hold on through the darkness and trust in God. God is holding me in the hollow of His hand; nothing can remove me from His strong right hand.

"My whole attitude toward God changed for good. I no longer look at people and let their problems define them. I want to give my life up to God more than keeping my everyday old life. Someone told me God does not make junk; He creates beauty from chaos.

"God said, 'Your Thoughts Are Valuable.'

"God smiles when He looks at me. He sees so much potential in me. If only I knew the thoughts God has for me, this would change my whole life. God does not keep these thoughts secret from me. Repeatedly in the Bible, He shares these with me. I read that He loves me and wants a personal relationship with me.

"Dealing with my emotional side opens a vast assortment of problems that I do not believe I can pack back into the can. Only God can take care of those loose worms. I asked myself, Is it safe and okay for me to exist? Do I tend to apologize for being alive? Can I use those feelings of no value and low self-esteem to praise my accomplishments and give myself credit for achievement in successful jobs and projects?

"God said, 'Do Not Fall in Love with the World.'

"Meet the very thing you fear directly, and you can master it. The deadly spider catches the fly in its web, resulting in death to innocence. Those who are wise do not have to be afraid but be cautious. I had to practice what I call 'fire drills' to be prepared for such encounters. I knew Jesus as my Lord and Savior and wanted my life to please Him. I was not strong enough to face these crises alone. Regardless of the temptation, the drill is the same. I had to take God's Word literally and flee temptation. I called out to Jesus at the first stirring of impure desire, saying to Him, 'Jesus, save me!' Then I focused with tunnel vision on Jesus holding me and comforting me as a father comforts his son when he is hurt. It works. I do not let Jesus out of my spiritual line of vision and stay within arm's reach of Him. He is the protector of the weak, senseless sheep wandering directly toward the enemy. With my spiritual ears, I repeatedly hear Jesus's voice, 'Do not be afraid; only believe.'

"God said, 'I Have Equipped You Fully.'

"When I need you to be on a mission for me, I will not send you out ill-prepared. I always equip my servants with all they need for the job I have for them. I will take care of everything. All I require of you is your willing heart to obey and trusting faith. I want you to listen carefully to these words that express God's thoughts to you and other chosen ones."

DR. SYDNEY: Today we will learn about what happened to you when you didn't get your needs met as a child.

If we experienced an unhealthy lifestyle, we have deficits that stay with us throughout life. We will blame our problems on somebody, and that somebody is usually God. "If you were a good God, you would not let this happen," or something similar. God had nothing to do with it. Humans used the freewill God gave them as a gift and rebelled against Him. That is why we have sin. Do you actually believe you can do a better job at running your life than God can? That kind of thinking quickly leads to more sin. Thinking like that got Lucifer thrown out of heaven and condemned to eternal fire.

It is okay to be angry. You need to acknowledge your anger and let it go, otherwise it will be like a cancer in your emotional and physical body. Anger and fear are thieves robbing you of peace and joy and good health.[26]

1. Every angry outburst follows a predictable progression, from buildup to explosion through a series of four stages. The good news is that each step provides an opportunity for derailing the person's anger once you've learned to recognize it.

2. Anger is often not a momentary event but a process, sometimes starting days, months, or even years before a blowup. Memories of sibling squabbles might cloud one's judgment so that one is remembering and fighting past wounds instead of the matter at hand in a moment of anger. What is perceived merely as an outburst of rage represents the culmination of a process that began elsewhere.

EVERY EPISODE OF ANGER PROGRESSES THROUGH FOUR LINKED STAGES: THE BUILDUP, THE SPARK, THE EXPLOSION, AND THE AFTERMATH.

https://blogs.psychcentral.com/unleash-creativity/2015/05/where-does-fear-come-from/ By Diana C. Pitaru, M.S., L.P.C. Last updated: 7 May 2015

STAGE ONE: THE BUILDUP

The buildup stage sets the foundation upon which the anger will be built. It is filled with memories of old, unresolved conflicts, poor problem-solving skills, and stresses of the person's age and stage of development. Hours, days, even months of tension can accumulate until the angry person can no longer take it.

STAGE TWO: THE SPARK

The spark is the action or thought that sets off the angry outburst. It may be big or small. It can be a thought, a feeling the child experiences, or an action by someone else. Kids respond differently to potential sparks. Some may react with rage, while some may not react at all.

The experiences in the buildup will influence how a child responds to a particular spark.

STAGE THREE: THE EXPLOSION

DR. GILLIAM USES A PARABLE TO ILLUSTRATE EMOTIONAL BOUNDARIES

Landmarks serve a purpose like stakes driven along your property line by a surveyor. When you connect them, you have a boundary that shows where your real estate stops, and someone else's starts. Without them, boundaries are unclear, often confused, and easily violated.

In ancient times piles of large round stones called "pylons" were used for the purpose, and sometimes they were disturbed, scattered, or even removed by enemies or adversaries. There are five verses of Scripture that refer to ancient landmarks, and one of them refers to a curse associated with disturbing or removing someone else's markers.

This parable applies to "emotional landmarks," and how vital they are in determining and defining your boundaries. Without them, your emotional boundaries will be unclear, often confused, sometimes enmeshed, and easily violated. As a result, emotional boundaries may become either too rigid of (the opposite) almost non-existent, and it will become challenging to know where to draw the line in relationships. The parable tells about a man who found that the stones which marked the edge of his property had been removed and scattered. He wondered how to replace the stones and how to determine where they used to be. Suddenly it began o rain. He noticed something strange nearby. Several little round pools of water started to form in the dents in the ground where the stones used to be. He then could tell where the stones should be replaced.

Next, imagine that the dents in the ground were filled, not with water, but with combustible fuel; this will help you understand how emotional landmarks become emotional landmines. The water is transformed into explosive fuel as a result of the pain and hurt you experienced when the stones were disturbed. You might even want to stop and think about what or who is most likely to ignite the fuel, detonate one of your emotional landmines, and trigger a "blow up." This information may provide important clues about how to dismantle or diffuse the mine, or how to "drain off" the fuel before trying to replace the landmark.

Most of the time behind the "what of who" that may trigger an emotional landmine, there is a perceived threat which ignites the fuel. This threat that is fuel is perpetuated by fear based on your false belief. Therefore, your false belief is perpetuated by fear, Then, this fear acts as fuel that is triggered by the perceived threat from your false belief sets off the explosion of the landmine. The explosion of the landmine is the result of your false belief and is the reason for us to change all our false beliefs to truth statements.

1. What "cues" triggered the perceived threat,

2. Whether the threat is actual or a "false alarm,"

3. Whether the fear is rational or irrational, and

4. Whether the belief behind it is true or false.

STAGE FOUR: THE AFTERMATH

We have witnessed people acting out with their anger in each one of these stages. No one is immune to anger, not even the President of the U.S.A. The following poem by Dr. Gilliam describes how the inner child acts out.

TO THE INNER C. E. O.

We walked along the surface of his maturity.
So professional, he seemed, and in control.
I admired his apparent confidence and security.
When suddenly, I stepped into a hole!
I do not know what I inadvertently disturbed,
But I could sense the deepness of the hole,
As something far below was primally perturbed.
And it rumbled through the caverns of his soul.
And I barely got my foot out and my leg away,
When volcanic pressure blew, belched, and spewed,
And I watched an impressive but spectacular display,
Which I neither comprehended, not understood.
What happened to the man mature with manner mild?
Why such eruption and smoldering residue?
And then I heard the whimper of a frightened child.
And I looked behind the tantrum, and I knew.
Four levels below intense anger and rage are fear.

Fear can be traced back to our knowledge of good and evil. Behind our feeling of injustice is anger. We desire to lash out at something, usually God. The angry thoughts of why God allowed this or that is false, because it was not God but his archenemy, Satan, but God gets the blame. And behind that false belief is that you should have stopped this __ (you fill in the blank with something, i.e., cancer, car accident, lost job) if you are a good God. When we become judge and jury, we are putting ourselves above God, and that has another false belief behind it.

If we examine our most significant problems—our anger, most profound sadness, anxieties, or most uncontrollable behaviors—we will always find an object of worship cracking its whip. Our problem is that we functionally worship other gods, taskmasters with whips in hand. But the God of the Bible is not like that, even though people have come up with their false ideas of who God is.

Rarely can we point to a single cause for problems in our lives.[27] They are usually complicated and can involve many people and events which impact us regularly. Compound these events over a lifetime, and it is no wonder that we are often at a loss to discern the root causes of such pressing issues. These many facets continually interact to make us who we are.

The four sources of our problems and their adverse effects on our lives are generational sins and curses, ungodly beliefs, life's hurts, and demonic oppression. There is a fundamental interrelatedness between each one and the other three sources. To bring lasting healing and freedom, one must receive ministry in the same general timeframe in all four areas. Understanding these truths and how they address the four sources will help us to move closer to the goal of becoming more and more like Jesus and living a life filled with joy and peace, regardless of our circumstances.

Our God Has a Generational Perspective

Our God is eternal. While we often focus on our here and now, God has a generational view of life. He is known throughout history as the God of Abraham, Isaac, and Jacob.

Down through the ages, God has honored family and heredity. As we love or honor God, He not only blesses us, but He also brings an inheritance of blessings to our children and grandchildren to a thousand generations. We call this Generational Blessings.

As we hate or dishonor God, our lives, and the lives around us suffer immensely. Over time and unchecked, our character and integrity become warped. That sin or iniquity can bring curses to us, our children, and our grandchildren to three or four generations. We call this Generational Sin.

As we understand God's perspective and His requirements, we can effectively deal with the generational sins and curses that have come into our lives through our family line. We can then intentionally pursue generational blessings not only for us, but also for our children and grandchildren.

Our God is the God of Truth

God cannot lie; His loving and holy perspective is always true. Jesus lived out that truth and perspective as an example for us to follow and know deep within our being. An essential key to our wholeness and freedom is receiving God's truth and applying it to the beliefs that guide our lives.

From the moment we enter this world, bits and pieces of information and impressions continually come together to form our beliefs and expectations. We consciously or subconsciously form opinions and make conclusions, but often these are wrong. No matter how staunchly we hold to and relentlessly defend them, they simply aren't correct. Developed over time, these ungodly beliefs seem reasonable to us based upon our life's facts and experiences. They affect our expectations and behavior (and others' behavior), which often lead to a cycle of reinforcing the ungodly beliefs, expectations, and resulting behavior.

There is a truth above the facts: God's truth. Gaining God's perspective and His truth about our life and experiences is essential. With it, we can understand our identity as God's beloved child and appropriate His healing and freedom in life. Our God is a God of truth.

Our God Heals Life's Hurts

God is our healer. He delights in healing us spiritually, emotionally, and physically. One of God's names is Jehovah Rapha—our God who heals.

The pain of past hurt can rule our lives. It simmers, it stifles, and sometimes it shuts us down entirely. Understanding scriptural principles brings comfort and hope, but it does not necessarily bring healing. Forgiveness releases us from bitterness and the bondage of negative ties to others, but it does not necessarily heal hurts. Demolishing demonic oppression brings great freedom, but it does not heal hurts.

God heals hurts. He is waiting and ready to touch our deepest pain if we will let Him. In a sense, His healing is another divine exchange in which we offer Him our hurt and we receive from Him His healing. Most of us do not know how to go about receiving this wonderful gift He has to offer.

Our God Sets His People Free

God is free, and that is His eternal character and desire for each of us. Our heavenly Father hates sin because it leads us into bondage and hinders our relationship with Him.

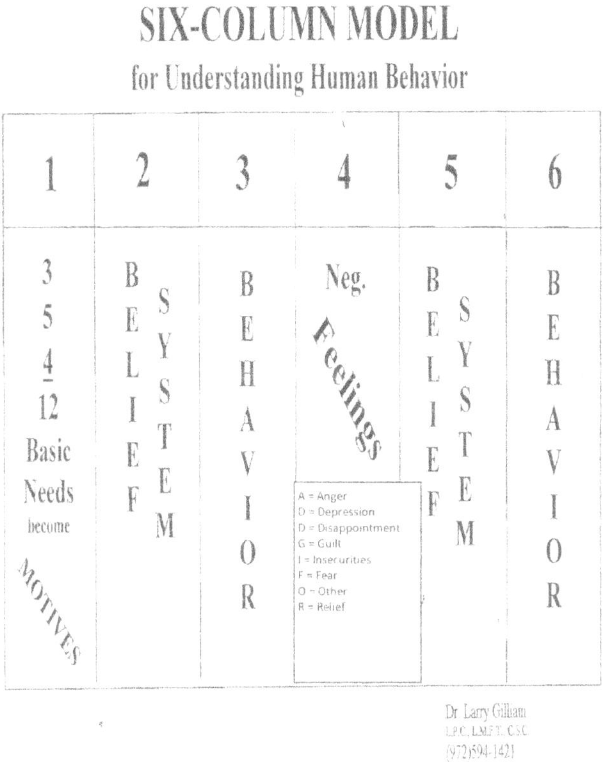

SIX-COLUMN MODEL
for Understanding Human Behavior

1	2	3	4	5	6
3 5 4 — 12 Basic Needs become *MOTIVES*	BELIEF SYSTEM	BEHAVIOR	Neg. *Feelings*	BELIEF SYSTEM	BEHAVIOR

A = Anger
D = Depression
D = Disappointment
G = Guilt
I = Insecurities
F = Fear
O = Other
R = Relief

Dr Larry Gilliam
LPC, LMFT, CSC
(972)594-1421

Column 1 of the Six-column Model for Understanding Human Behavior regards 12 emotions that become motives. Emotion means coming out of, or from motor, motion, motive – doing something. The purpose is what motivates you. These 12 things you need and seek include:

The number 3 in Column 1: Three things or feelings, or the evidence of these, you find intently, which you feel you need, want, expect, feel entitled to or feel you deserve, including belongingness and acceptance, are also factors in our self-image;

The number 5 in Column 1: Five underlying fears you seek to avoid, including engulfment, abandonment and rejection, and

The number 4 in Column 1: Four things you do to find relief. These are automatic responses that you don't think about, internal programs related to survival.

Column 2 concerns what you actually believe about getting stuff in Col 1. How do you know? How you feel and what you do tell your belief system.

Column 3 includes behavior in keeping with Col 2, feelings, words, and actions. If the behavior "works," you have positive feelings, peace, joy, etc.

Column 4 relates to negative feelings of Anger, Guilt, Depression, insecurities, Relief, Disappointment, Fear, and other.

These negative feelings result when Column 3 behavior, is spurred on by Column 2 beliefs, about how to attain Column 1 needs fail. These feelings include anger, depression, disappointment, fears, and guilt. There are ten symptoms of social and emotional guilt: Over sensitiveness, 2. Anxiety, 3. Sadness, 4. Fear of new opportunities, 5. Making wrong decisions, 6. Avoiding their emotions, 7. Lacking self-esteem, 8. Lack of focus for aims and purposes, 9. They become hurdle in their success, 10, Become more offensive. When you experience any of these as an issue, there are only three things to do:

1. Continue to follow the behavior and experience the feelings of guilt,

2. Become a victim. Figure out a way to get punished, hoping someday you will feel you've been punished enough, and:

   A. Punish and sabotage yourself or,

   B. Arrange for someone else to do it, causing others to hurt you.

3. You can deal with the issue. Column 5 relates to dealing with things because you don't feel right. How can I handle these painful emotions?" your belief system will tell you what to do. You cannot plug the hole till you get back to your belief system.

Column 6 (or Column 2) – The extent to which reality does not match our expectations, on a scale of 1 to 10, if you have hopes of 8 and reality of 4. Four units of energy are bouncing around in our system.

Are all of your beliefs now aligned with scripture? If not, you will not progress. So go back and align all your beliefs with scripture; you will move to column six when that is done.

MOTIVES.XLS

(NEARLY ALL HUMAN BEHAVIOR CAN BE EXPLAINED BY THIS MODEL)				
EVERY HUMAN'S MOTIVES	KEY ELEMENTS	EXPERIENCED BY	RANK	FROM WHOM OR WHAT?
A. *Seeking for feelings of / evidence of:*	(Bonding)			
1. Belongingness	Personal Connection	Intimacy		
2. Self Worth	Importance	(Six Ways)		
3. Competence	Approval	Positive Feedback		
B. *Seeking to avoid feelings of fear of*				
4. Rejection	Acceptance	Warm Kind Words		
5. Abandonment	Attention	Warm Affectionate Touch		
6. Pain / Pain Memory	Tolerance	Smiles, Body Language		
7. Engulfment	Respect	Space and a Place		
8. Fear of Fear	Safety	Protection		
C. *Obtaining relief or safety through automatic or reactionary resonses*				
9. Survival	Perceived Threat	Safe place/safe people		
10. Internal Programs	Understanding	Freedom from "Negative Cues"		
11. Sensual Pleasure	Physical Contact	Food, sex etc.		
12. Spiritual Conviction	Peace	Freedom from guilt (spirit filledness)		
It is not good for a person to be alone (Gen 2:18)				
Which of these 'motives' drives you the most?				
To whom or what do you look to satisfy these motives?				
"Ye do err..." (Why?) Two reasons. (See Matt 22:29 and Mark 12:24)				
(These two reasons explain why people keep doing the same hurtful, unhealthy, unproductive things over and over.)				

Are you trying to avoid emotions of fear of rejection, abandonment, engulfment, or fear of fear? Then it would help if you had acceptance and warm, kind words spoken to you.

a) If you seek to avoid the fear of rejection, you need a safe place and safe people.

b If you seek to avoid the fear of abandonment, you need attention and warm, affectionate touch.

c) If you seek to avoid the fear of engulfment, you need respect and space and a place you feel you belong.

d) If you seek to avoid the fear of fear, you need safety and protection.

If you need relief or safety through automatic or reactionary responses, you need survival, internal programs, sensual pleasure, or spiritual conviction.

a) If you seek relief or safety from the threats, you need a safe place and safe people.

b) If you seek relief or safety from damaging internal programs of anger, depression, disappointment, guilt, insecurities, or fear, you need to change the negative self-talk to positive self-talk.

c) If you seek relief or safety from sensual pleasure, you need appropriate physical contact, food, sex, and others.

d) If you seek relief or safety from spiritual conviction, you need peace and freedom from guilt.

Did you resolve each item in your belief system? If not, you must go back and examine your true or false statements and align them with Scripture. You will not change your behavior until you do.

If you did not reconcile the problem, you need to look at roots of bitterness that are still in your heart, or generational patterns. Do more work on reparenting the inner child because there are always false beliefs that must be changed to truths.

Instead of feeling rejected, do you feel you belong, cared for, part of a family? If your behavior changed, then you were successful in changing the negative to a positive. If not, who are you blaming? You still have that false belief.

Instead of feeling guilty, do you feel you count, are okay, necessary to someone, and that someone is important to you? If not, who are you blaming? You still have that false belief.

Instead of feeling a lack of competence, do you feel important and have positive feedback? If not, who are you blaming? You still have that false belief.

Deficits for Father, Older Brother, Mother

1. Sense of belonging comes from your father.
2. Sense of self-worth comes from your older brother or your favorite uncle.
3. Sense of competence comes from your mother.

If there were deficits, you will set about to find someone to fill the vacuum.

Deficits Cause Feelings:

1. Anger, hostility, and rejection—you will find someone to blame.
2. Guilt, at fault when it is not your fault—you blame yourself.
3. Fearful and insecure—you tend to blame God or your concept of who runs the universe. You will either think of God as a therapist or a rapist. To think of God as a rapist, you are those at Jesus's trial

calling for His crucifixion. God calls you a fool and describes you in Psalm 14, because you blame Him for your problems, not realizing you are the guilty party. God had nothing to do with human suffering. It was man's rebellion against God that brought sin to humanity. God is good, and if He gave you what you think you deserve, remember, the only thing humans deserve from God is death.

Self-image is influenced by not filling the vacuum caused by feelings.

Where Do Our Thoughts Come From

There is a big-mouth, know-it-all, critical judge in your head who condemns you each time you don't meet your goal. You know, the one who is quick to say: "I am not good enough," "This will not work," "You are stupid." That one must be silenced at all costs. Kick him out and replace him with Mr. Positive Affirmation, who tells you, "I am somebody, I can do this, I love you." The little voices in our heads are thoughts we continuously repeat to ourselves.

When we try to control these thoughts, we quickly realize this guy is more muscular than we realized. He will not go with outside pressure; you must go where he is in the subconscious and mentally drag him out, kicking and screaming. God has given us the power to capture every thought. Ask God to give you help if you need it. While you are cleaning house, kick out his roommates too.

"When the unclean spirit comes out of a person, it passes through waterless places seeking rest and does not find it. Then it says, 'I will return to my house from which I came,' and when it comes, it finds it unoccupied, swept, and put in order. Then it goes and brings along with it seven other spirits more wicked than itself, and they come in and live there, and the last condition of that person becomes worse than the first. That is the way it will also be with this evil generation" (Matthew 12:43–45).

Just as there are biological pathogens like bacteria, viruses, and parasites, there are nonphysical pathogens in etheric parasites, discarnate humans, aliens, and demonic beings that can attach themselves to a living person, drain their energy, and influence their thoughts, feelings, and personality.[28]

Thoughts originate from the subconscious mind. To change our thoughts, we must do so in the subconscious. Our thoughts stimulate our imagination, and our imagination is the source of everything we create. And that is what makes changing our thought processes so hard. To make it easier, we must initiate the change where these thoughts originate from: the subconscious mind.

Our thoughts consist of electrical energy that continually flows through the human mind. Nothing gets done without a person first thinking about it. Thinking is a mental activity that never ceases; there is no beginning or end. Thus, our thoughts are the rational expression of the electrical energy flowing through our minds.

The ability to think is one of the ten communicable gifts in our DNA that God gave humans at creation. We do not usually choose our thoughts; they appear from the constant flow of mental chatter. Each person has the power to control their thoughts and consciously choose how they think.

We need to understand how to use our thoughts for our good and the good of others. When we are aware of our thoughts, we can accept or reject those that do not fit our view of who we are or want to be. We must be conscious of past thoughts that are no longer needed. These may sabotage your current plans for moving toward a healthy beginning. Reject every thought based on your old thinking and only allow new ones that are not predictable that look like the present. Remember, you want to change, and you will never change by following that old familiar pattern. New action demands new thinking. You can accept or reject any thought.

God's communicable attributes that He gave humans when He imprinted His image on man are part of how we get thoughts. Other thoughts come from our five senses. God's communicable attributes are wisdom, knowledge, power, holiness, righteousness, justice, jealousy, wrath, goodness, love, and mercy. You can trace their origin by starting with how you feel, identifying the thoughts that sparked that emotion, and taking note of the circumstances where your thoughts and feelings conspired to bring on a subsequent self-sabotaging behavior or action.

Pretty soon you will start to notice specific patterns. Perhaps your thoughts tend to catastrophize what happens to you, and your mind goes straight to the worst-case scenario, no matter how unlikely it is. Or perhaps you make a lot of rules with your thoughts, a lot of "shoulds," and that has you believing you don't measure up, no matter how hard you try. Or maybe your thoughts attempt to mind-read a situation and other people, where you believe you know what others might be thinking about you. In doing so, you inadvertently betray some of your deepest insecurities.

You can take power back, build self-efficacy, and regain control of the process so these bothersome thoughts do not inevitability lead to self-sabotage. You choose your thoughts. These, in turn, cause your feelings or emotions, which then lead to your actions. Our motivation drives our behavior. Our emotions affect that behavior. Emotions can result from situations where our motives and goals are satisfied, threatened, or frustrated.

Emotions occur from the motive itself and are the driving force for our behavior. Emotions are event-driven, which is a learned behavior. The motive and emotions rely on the relationship between the individual and his environment. Emotions are feelings or affective experiences that are shaped in response to specific stimuli. An emotion is a mental and physiological feeling that directs our attention and guides our behavior. Emotions and motives are linked together and activate or energize behavior. Both are made up of energy. The purpose of emotions is to communicate with others.

Our memories, thoughts, and beliefs create emotions, as the brain will interpret what is going on around us and in our lives. Emotions then trigger how we feel or behave. All our decisions in life are influenced in some way by this process. Emotions can affect the nature of the decision we make and the speed at which we make it.

"Keep your thoughts positive because your thoughts become your words. Keep your words positive because your words become your behavior. Keep your behavior positive because your behavior becomes your habits. Keep your habits positive because your habits become your values. Keep your values positive because your values become your destiny."—Mahatma Gandhi

Infants arrive highly prepared to face life, learn, and grow.[29] They are brilliant, voracious learners on the lookout for need-relevant information. Then, as infants try to meet their needs, something important happens. They start building beliefs about their world and their role in it: Is the world good or bad, safe, or dangerous? Can I count on my world to meet my needs? These beliefs, plus the emotions and action tendencies that are stored with them, are termed "BEATs." They represent the accumulated experiences people have had trying to meet their needs. They play a crucial role in both the invisible and visible parts of the personality. The invisible part consists of the person's needs and BEATs. They form the basis of personality, and they drive and guide the visible part. The visible part happens when the needs and BEATs create the actual goals people pursue in the world—what people do.

What are the implications of this? First, it means that our personality develops around our motivations (our needs and goals) and is not merely about traits we have at birth. It also reveals the invisible parts of personality and shows how we can identify and address essential BEATs (particularly beliefs) to promote personality change, what happens to you when you do not get your needs met as a child. If we experienced an unhealthy lifestyle, we have deficits that stay with us throughout life.[30]

When I talk about the inner child, Jerry, I am not talking about a physical child. "Inner child" is the name given to the childhood emotions that were damaged and locked away in your subconscious. Your wounded emotions from childhood are buried in your subconscious mind, and most of the time you are unaware of them.

Your body posture is revealing. When you walk with your shoulders rounded and head down, your body language tells me you have unresolved emotional and physical pain. Your body remembers! Other body language that tells me the same thing is lack of a smile and no twinkle in the eye, and laughter.

You may wonder where the inner child is located within you. The following illustrations will make this clear. Picture in your mind a four-drawer chest. The four drawers represent your subconscious, conscious, pre-conscious, and unconscious. The inner child may be in any drawer at any given time, but mostly he hangs out in the subconscious. This whole thing about the inner child is all about thoughts with feelings. Since our motive for learning how our thoughts work is to uncover the wrong motives we have and the false beliefs behind them, we will continue with several more sessions looking at our thoughts.

Our feelings show up in how we say things and in our nonverbal body language. This morning we are looking at these forms of communication.

The body plays a role in communicating something about how we're feeling. Our faces, postures, and the way we walk can give subtle hints to an observant onlooker. All the knowledge you need to interpret body language is stored safely in your subconscious mind. Some of it will have been downloaded from your DNA, though you may have lost touch with part of it.

When speaking, the tone, speed, and passion you express with the words are revealed. But when reading, the tone, speed, and passion are hidden under the surface, out of sight. The author intends to convey the actual feelings. In reverse, the sentences a person says do not convey the hidden, under the surface. Still, plainly in sight, the person's intent is expressed in his body language. Therefore, body language is about feelings in the subconscious that speak the truth. Most people are unaware that their body is speaking its language, or, if they are aware, what their bodies are saying.[31]

People are born with the skills needed for interpreting body language. Here are some tips:

1. Don't focus on just one sign out of context, as it may be misleading.

2. Look for clusters of body-language signs.

3. Consider cultural differences in gestures and movement.

4. Continue to increase your self-awareness.

5. Always check how your feelings have potentially influenced your interpretation.

Emotions are like signs on the highway that communicate invaluable insight to us. People who pay attention to these signs lead happier lives, while people who ignore their emotional signs may end up lost. Emotions always serve a function, such as providing information about a situation or motivating us to act. The best approach to take with our emotions is to acknowledge them, accept them, and learn from them.

Sometimes our emotions can lead us astray. For instance, you might feel guilty about taking care of yourself or feel anxious at a party. The thing is, with emotional problems, our thermostat, so to speak, often becomes too sensitive, meaning that we start to feel these emotions when they're not warranted. Emotion regulation is the ability to exert control over one's emotional state.[32] It may involve behaviors such as rethinking a challenging situation to reduce anger or anxiety, hiding visible signs of sadness or fear, or focusing on reasons to feel happy or calm.

Two broad categories of emotion regulation are reappraisal—changing how one thinks about something that prompted an emotion to change one's response—and suppression, which has been linked to more negative outcomes. Other strategies include selecting or changing a situation to influence one's emotional experience, shifting what one pays attention to, and trying to accept emotions.

Practicing habits such as mindful acceptance of emotions, shifting attention away from the source of negative emotions, or reframing emotional situations (such as thinking about a setback or mistake as an opportunity to learn) may be helpful, and a trained therapist could be a valuable partner in enhancing emotional control.

What are the most challenging emotions to control? The negative ones—anger, depression, disappointment, guilt, insecurities, and fear—are difficult to control.

Many of us aren't particularly good at listening to our emotions. Practice this mindfulness exercise regularly to become more aware of your thoughts and emotions in a more general sense. Imagine you are standing at the door of a castle wall. As the gatekeeper, you oversee who comes and goes through that door. What comes through that door isn't people, though, but your thoughts and feelings, and you're going to decide which ones get to come in. If they come to the door, they need to be let in or they'll make camp outside that door and continue to bang on it harder and harder. Instead, the idea is that you greet each thought and feeling as it enters, simply acknowledging its presence before the next thought or feeling arrives. You accept each experience as it comes. "Anger is at the door," "Here is sadness," "Here is a thought about the past," and "Here comes anger again," and so on.

By noting each experience, acknowledging what has come up for you, that thought or emotion will pass through the door rather than hang around. It might come back repeatedly, but you will see that it doesn't stay long; it just passes through, and then the next experience arises. When we accept our emotions, we open ourselves to listening to them, and to ourselves, without judgment.

No one in the world can think or read your thoughts for you. This is one of the unique things that sets us apart from animals or angels. Only God knows your thoughts, and He has a book with your name on it with every detail of information, including every thought, recorded in it. He has one on every individual. (Psalm 139)

Uncovering and examining your automatic thoughts can reveal some essential ideas established in your past that continue to trigger your self-sabotaging behavior in the present. Next time you feel a distressing or painful emotion, ask yourself, "What did I think just before I noticed this emotion?"

What precedes emotions? Thoughts and events do not take on a specific meaning until you attribute thoughts to them. The critical thing to notice here is how self-sabotaging triggers don't just come out of nowhere.[33]

Techniques to Erase Subconscious Negativity

"As you sow in your subconscious mind, so shall you reap in your body and environment."—Joseph Murphy

The subconscious mind is like a computer's hard drive. It saves whatever information you feed it, without any bias. It does not discriminate between useful information and trash information. It just saves everything!

The subconscious mind learns through repetition. So if it's fed the same information multiple times, it keeps overwriting it until the information gets etched in. For example, let's say you write, "I am not good enough" on a piece of paper. Now keep writing over the top of that. The more you write, the bolder the text becomes and the harder it is to erase later. Yes, it is erasable, but erasing it would require extra effort. This is precisely why bad habits are so difficult to break.

Let's look at another example. When you first learned to ride a bicycle, you found it hard to balance. But you kept trying and could maintain balance for five seconds and then ten seconds and so on. Finally, you could maintain balance for more extended periods. Because of the repetition, your subconscious mind picked up what it takes to maintain balance. Once the subconscious mind learns, it falls back on this information whenever it is required. When information is fed to the subconscious mind and repeated enough times, it gets etched in the mind and is hard to erase later.

Awareness is a habit, and the more you practice it, the more it becomes second nature.

1. Consciously watch your thoughts. The goal is to detach from your thoughts for a few moments and watch them as a neutral observer.

2. Consciously feel your emotions. Becoming aware of your emotions helps you understand the thought-emotion connection; in other words, what kinds of thoughts produce what kinds of emotional responses in your body.

    What I find works best is to recreate emotional responses when you are by yourself, consciously. Let's say certain situations cause intense anxiety in you. What you are doing here is becoming aware of thought patterns and the reactions they create in your body.

3. Consciously feel your body. Becoming aware of your body can help you learn how to relax, and thereby aid healing. Relaxing your body is key to healing.

4. Consciously focus your attention. With practice, you can learn to change the spontaneous flow of words going through your brain (i.e., your thoughts are your internal dialogue). You can do this by challenging the logic underlying your negative ideas; coming up with alternative explanations for situations and other people's behaviors; changing the stories that you tell yourself about the past, the world, and your relationships; continually practice giving yourself positive and affirming messages and encouragement.

It is essential to clarify what happened in the past to understand how you developed your style of perceiving, thinking, feeling, and behaving (your attachment style) in adulthood. Once you understand where it came from, you can see that your style is regular, and you can stop blaming yourself for having it. This, in turn, will give you the freedom to change those aspects of your personality to be a healthy you.

Emotions are your body's reaction to what you are thinking, whether you're thinking on purpose or not. Your belief system and other subconscious thoughts are happening on autopilot all the time, and they often cause emotions. That's why sometimes you have no idea why you feel the way you do.

Self-sabotage is when we actively or passively take steps to prevent ourselves from reaching our goals. This behavior can affect nearly every aspect of life, be it a relationship, a career goal, or a personal goal such as weight loss. Although quite common, it is an incredibly frustrating cycle of behavior that lowers our self-confidence and leaves us feeling stuck. There are many reasons someone may choose to self-sabotage, but most stem from a lack of belief in ourselves.

1. We lack self-worth.

2. We fear success.

3. We want to place fault elsewhere.

4. We want to control.

Fill your heart with love instead of bitterness because love drives out fear. Just like darkness flees from the light, so fear flees from love. Love is something you give, and by giving love, you get it back again so you can give it again.

Never Underestimate the Power of Fear

Fear is the result of becoming fixated on images of an undesirable situation we fear will happen to us. Fear is the mind projecting within itself images of what it does not want to happen. If the fear is not recognized and dealt with early on, it can and will find root within our consciousness. When this happens, fear then becomes a daily occurrence. If these thoughts are repeated, they will eventually make an imprint on a subconscious level. Then the subconscious mind begins to attract the same experiences we have been projecting. It is an example of how our minds work so effectively, even when we unwittingly use it against ourselves. Why am I projecting images in my mind of events that I don't want to happen? Never underestimate the power of fear. Unless people can change their fear of losing to an expectation of winning, their chances of winning are slim to none.

Overcome Self-Sabotage[34]

1. Become a self-sabotage detective. First, identify self-sabotaging actions and behaviors.

   a)   Identify the triggers.

   b)   Notice your critical inner voice. Write down your thoughts.

   c)   Watch out for subtle, internal self-talk. What can I say to myself right now that is positive and encouraging?

2. Make your internal self-talk work for you. It is fear that drives that internal, critical voice.

3. Replace negative behaviors with positive ones.

4. Make the unknown more known. Behind every uncertainty is an uncomfortable feeling of fear and anxiety.

   a)   Set clear goals and plans.

   b)   Create a step-by-step road map to follow.

   c)   Start with doing those steps.

   d)   Identify anything on your list that seems complicated.

   e)   Visualize reselecting confidently and seeing things go the way you want them to.

5. Boost your self-worth.

The problem is that these thoughts are sometimes not based on current logic but stem from our childhood, from a time when a different logic was applied.

The fear of spiders is an excellent example of dislodging negative entity attachments. A fear of spiders can come from childhood. We might have watched one of our parents scream frantically and jump on a chair when they saw a spider. That's when our subconscious mind learned spiders are dangerous and something to be afraid of. This logic made sense to us when we were a child. Now, as an adult, we know most spiders are not dangerous. And even though this adult logic makes sense to us, we are probably still afraid of spiders because this adult logic does not apply to our subconscious mind.

The Three Things You Need to Develop Your Clarity of Purpose[35]

First, define what success means to you personally. Second, create a vivid mental image of you as a success. This image should be as vivid as you can make it. Third, clarify your values.

"Clarity keeps you from boredom!"—Kim Basinger

Session 8—Our Core Beliefs

Dr. Sydney: As a person thinks, so is he (Proverbs 23:7 paraphrased). You may wonder why I am beginning our time like this. In all our counseling sessions, we've considered who we are and how we got this way. The genuine cause of our problems is what is in our hearts; this is the description of how God summed up the human heart's natural condition, the place of our thoughts.

Clarence L. Haynes Jr. said one of the unique gifts God gave us is the human mind.[36] The ability to learn, think, choose, and reason is the essence of what makes us human. While the ability to think makes us human, it goes deeper. Your thoughts become a reflection of who you are. God certainly understands this, and He speaks to it in various places throughout His Word.

"For as he thinks within himself, so he is. He says to you, 'Eat and drink!' But his heart is not with you" (Proverbs 23:7).

The root of who we are is in the heart because our words come from our thoughts, and thoughts are in the heart. It matters significantly, because our thoughts shape our words and shape our actions that form the basis of who we will become.

Who you are on the inside and what you say on the outside don't always line up. For example, the Pharisees were exceptionally good at presenting themselves as pious, devout, religious people, yet Jesus called them hypocrites. The word "hypocrite" in Greek means actor. The Pharisees were playing a role on the outside that did not reflect who they were.

Jesus said you would know a tree by its fruit. The fruit of the tree is simply a reflection of the root to which it is connected. You will never get an orange from an apple-tree root. The core of who you are is evidenced by the thoughts, or roots, of your heart. That is why what is on the inside is so much more important than what is on the outside. You can mask the outside to others and you can try to bury it in the world around you, but ultimately, what is in your heart will reveal who you are.

The root or core meaning of this verse is one of hypocrisy. You say one thing, but you do not mean it. It is like the unethical salesperson who will tell you how wonderful you look in that outfit only to make the sale. The bottom line is, God hates hypocrisy.

Are You Serving Out of a Relationship or for Acceptance?

"Not everyone who says to Me, 'Lord, Lord,' will enter the kingdom of heaven, but he who does the will of My Father, who is in heaven, will enter. Many will say to Me on that day, 'Lord, Lord, did we not prophesy in Your name, and in Your name cast out demons, and in Your name perform many miracles?' I will then declare to them that I never knew you; depart from Me, you who practice lawlessness" (Matthew 7:21–23).

What is fascinating about this Scripture is that people are not evil; they were not flowing out of a relationship with Christ, which is terrible. It was like they were using the things they did to gain favor or win God's approval. The way to the Father is through Jesus Christ. Any other way is evil, even though we do not often think of it in these terms.

If you are serving, then let your service to Him flow out of your relationship with Him. You serve Him because you love Him. You do not serve Him to get Him to love you.

"Beware of practicing your righteousness before men to be noticed by them; otherwise, you have no reward with your Father, who is in heaven" (Matthew 6:1).

Jesus jumps straight to the heart of the matter: Why are you doing what you are doing? You might claim you are doing it for the right reason. Jesus is encouraging us to be careful of the why, because when you know that, it reveals what's really in your heart.

"As you think, so are you. Watch over your heart with all diligence, for from it flows the springs of life" (Proverbs 4:23).

Vigilance is defined as the action or state of keeping careful watch for possible danger or difficulties. That is exactly what God calls us to do with our hearts. We are to pay extra attention to our hearts and watch them closely. There will be dangers and difficulties we will face in this life, and we should be ready.

The springs of life are our thinking, feeling, and choosing; these are what are inside our heart that come out of our heart.

Seven Ways to Guard Your Heart[37]

1. Protect everything that comes in. What influences us are what we think about, what we see, hear, or read. We need to use wisdom in what we allow into our hearts. Train your eyes to look away from lust. Listen to wisdom instead of folly.

2. Persevere in the face of difficulties. Difficulties and suffering are part of life.

3. Follow what the Lord is leading you to do. What is God asking you to do? What do you desire and cannot stop thinking about?

4. Cultivate an atmosphere of community. We need people. We need community.

5. Keep priorities high and do not compromise.

6. Trust the Lord with the rest.

7. Preach the Gospel to yourself each day. The second we take our eyes off the cross, we forget who we are. Our hearts need to be reminded that while we still sin, we are forgiven, redeemed, and are children of God! As you start your day with this truthful reminder, you will have no choice but to glorify God in everything you do, because you will find it so ridiculous that you get to do anything at all!

How Can I Reclaim Areas of My Life that I Surrendered to Satan?[38]

1. Ask the Holy Spirit to bring to remembrance every instance we have given ground to Satan through moral impurity, bitterness, and greed.

2. Confess each sin that the Holy Spirit brings to remembrance—1 John 1:9.

3. Claim the blood of Jesus—Revelation 12:11.

4. Ask the Lord to restore your soul and regain the ground you have given to Satan—Psalm 23:3. What ground have you given to Satan that needs to be regained?

5. Pull down every stronghold (the false idea) and put on the truth from God's Word—2 Corinthians 10:3–5.

Psychologist Dr. Carsten Wrosch has studied bitterness for fifteen years. He says, "When harbored for a long time, bitterness may forecast biological deregulation (a physiological impairment that can affect metabolism, immune response, or organ function) and physical disease. Scientists have concluded that bitterness, if left unchecked, interferes with the body's hormonal and immune systems. Bitter people tend to have higher blood pressure and heart rate and are much more likely to die of heart disease and other illnesses."[39]

Of course, the apostle Paul did not have access to this scientific data when he wrote much of the New Testament, but that didn't keep him from connecting the dots between bitterness and our bodies. In Acts 8:23, Paul describes the gall of bitterness as bile, a bitter substance that can make us sick.

I have a friend who regularly visits nursing homes to serve communion to the infirm. On multiple occasions, she has told me that she can walk into such settings and identify bitter women by merely looking at them. Their postures and expressions cannot help but betray the bitterness that has burrowed deep into their hearts.

Indeed, not all physical ailments are the fruit of a bitter root, but some are. Is it possible that the cells of your body are wilting under the weight of unchecked bitterness?

The bitter root in Hebrews 12:15 is first described in Deuteronomy 29:18: "Beware lest there be among you a man or woman or clan or tribe whose heart is turning away today from the LORD our God to go and serve the gods of those nations. Beware lest there be among you a root bearing poisonous and bitter fruit."

Like all weeds, bitterness has a way of spreading. This passage describes one possible progression. A man infects his wife; she infects her children. The bitterness spreads, and soon the whole tribe is infected. Is it possible that your bitterness has had a ripple effect and that the poisonous root has burrowed past your own heart and into the hearts of the people you love?

A root is like a bubbling fountain lying under the surface. Roots do not directly manifest or make themselves known but are a source of nutrition or fuel for other elements that are on the surface. You do not usually see a plant showing off its root system, but if the plant did not have a root system, it would not survive. A root's job is not to manifest on the surface but to brew underneath and fuel things on the surface.

Let's take a closer look at a plant's root system. Where do the roots dwell? Under the surface of the soil. Can we see its root system? No, because it is hidden. The same is true with bitterness in a person's soul. It is a hidden element that lies under the surface, and out of it springs up anger and other negative emotions against others and the circumstances around us. People who have a root of bitterness find it easy to get upset over things others are doing around them. It is like a brewing fountain that lies beneath the surface, waiting to feel something on the surface.[40]

Countless women who are raped develop awful emotional and spiritual bondage. It is not because they were raped, but because they allowed the trauma to get to them. Today, many women are in bondage because they became bitter under the surface about what was done to them years ago.

Clinton Clark once said that it seemed boys molested by older men, who forgave the molester and forgot about it right away, walked away without picking up unclean gay spirits, but those who allowed the trauma to bother them walked away with gay spirits and other bondages. That is how demonic spirits gain access to a person's life through rape and abuse.[41]

Often a person who has been taken advantage of through abuse or rape lets bitter and other unhealthy feelings build up in their heart. Demons thrive on bitterness and unforgiveness, and it is a wide-open door for them to move right in on a person and develop many spiritual, mental, and even physical bondages.

Many people who have been hurt do not express it on the outside but hold the hurt and bitter feelings inside, where they fester and grow. I know women who have been raped, and they are kind and gentle and loving people, but inside they are bound up because of what was done to them many years ago. Just because they are not angry or outrageous individuals does not mean they are free from the root of bitterness. As I said earlier, bitterness is a root, and roots are not always visible on the surface. They may promote ungodly anger.

Other emotions are on the surface, but bitterness works underneath. Since bitterness is a root, it is harder to identify and expose than many other issues, but it is a deadly poison that needs to be released. If left alone, it will grow and fester, and it can spring up issues such as irritability, anger, hatred, etc. Individuals who have a root of bitterness will often find it easy to become upset over little things around them. It is easy for them to look at the circumstances as the source of their problems rather than see how they handle those circumstances. Instead of letting go and forgiving, they let it get to them, and it devours them alive. This is a prevalent route by which demons enter people today.

Whether bitterness is manifested on the outside or not doesn't matter. If there is a root of bitterness, it needs to be cut off and removed from one's soul. We need to choose to release all hurt and bottled-up feelings inside our systems and repent for holding that poison in our hearts. Turn from those feelings and forsake them, and allow the Lord's love to minister to your soul!

The Germination

The seed of bitterness is a hurt planted in someone. It may be intentional or unintentional. Someone does not mean to hurt you, but you were hurt. Sometimes the hurt is only imagined: no one has hurt you, but somehow you feel someone has done something wrong to you. There are also times when the hurt may be the very chastisement of God upon your life.

The soil of bitterness is a heart that harbors hostility and does not deal with hurt by the grace of God. When someone becomes bitter, the bitterness takes root in the heart and grows more profound.

The world is full of people who have not dealt with an old hurt. They look for things to criticize, people to find fault with, and ways to justify the way they feel. Have you ever seen hypercritical people? Generally, they are bitter people. They know how to push your hot buttons until you react in a way to justify their bitterness further. Then they can say, "Aha! I was right. I have a right to be bitter." We Need to Take Bitterness Seriously.

Every good gardener knows that you cannot chop weeds. Try to go after crabgrass with a weed eater and you will get nowhere in a hurry; you have to rip weeds up by the roots. Otherwise, they will keep coming back, and when they do, they are bound to bring more and more of their weedy friends. It is no accident that God uses the image of a weed to describe a particular sin that has a way of creeping into all our hearts: bitterness.

Bitterness is not one of those big, flashy sins you can see growing on the surface of our hearts. It may not show off like anger or produce rotten fruit like disobedience. Bitterness is a sleeper sin growing beneath the surface, down deep in the soil of our hearts.

Hebrews is clear that the bitter root will one day sprout, and when it does, many will become defiled. If that bitter root keeps growing, there will be a harvest of pain for you and the people in your world. And because bitterness is a weedy sin that burrows in our hearts first, we cannot just cut off the behaviors it causes. We need the Lord's help to yank that destructive weed up by its root.

A. If we do not deal with bitterness, it will progress toward extreme anger (wrath).

B. If we do not deal with the anger, we will start to clamor or demand what we want.

C. If that does not work, we will start to talk bad about the object of our bitterness in the hope of recruiting others to agree with and justify our feelings (slander).

D. If that goes unchecked, we will eventually desire to harm that person.

All along the way, people are hurt, relationships are derailed, joy is stolen, and growth of the fruit of the Spirit is stunted. With so much on the line, it is wise to ask ourselves often, Am I bitter?

You Get More Than Bitterness, The Gang that Bitterness Travels In:

In Ephesians 4:31–5:2, Paul describes a cluster of emotions that come along with bitterness. I know from experience that bitterness almost always travels in a nasty pack, including wrath, anger, clamor, slander, and malice. All these make life stink, and others with sensitive noses can smell the rottenness. Which would you rather smell like, a rotten potato or a rose?

You cannot hide bitterness and its friends. Your spouse, children, or an intimate friend knows. You are fooling only yourself. These are progressive emotions that quickly spread. The opposite of progressive emotions is sleeper sins.

The Devastation and Fruit of Bitterness—What Does It Affect?

We have learned about the seed and the soil of bitterness, now let us look at the root and the fruit of bitterness found in our text from Hebrews 12:14–15.

The root of bitterness is underground; it is easy to hide and camouflage. Seldom do you find anyone who will admit to being a bitter person; they will either deny it or disguise it. A bitter person is hypersensitive, ungrateful, insincere, holds grudges, and has mood swings.

The Fruit of Bitterness: bitterness will affect you physically, emotionally, and spiritually, because the fruit of bitterness is an acid that destroys its container. When your heart is bitter, God will not be real to you. Why? Because hatefulness and holiness do not dwell in the same heart. And without holiness, you will not see the Lord.

The Eradication of Bitterness—How to Get Rid of the Root

There are three steps to eradicating bitterness:

A. Let God Reveal It. Sometimes people say, "I know my heart; there is no bitterness in me." The truth is you don't know your heart. God's Word tells us, "The heart is deceitful above all things, and desperately wicked: who can know it?" (Jeremiah 17:9). A deceitful heart cannot diagnose a deceitful heart. You need to let the Holy Spirit do radical surgery.

B. Let Grace Reveal It. A response of bitterness is never right when someone has done something wrong to you. You need to ask God to forgive you. If someone has wronged you, cut it down and forget it. By the grace of God, bury that hurt in the grave of God's forgetfulness. Justice is God giving us what we deserve; mercy is God not giving us what we deserve; grace is God giving us what we do not deserve.

C. Let Good Replace It. Hebrews 12:14 says, "Follow peace with all men, and holiness, without which no man shall see the Lord." You cannot be holy unless you follow peace with men. It is so worth it when you forgive. But, you say, "Look what they've done! I am not going to let them off the hook." Well, they are not on the hook; you are! When you forgive, you set two people free, and one of them is yourself.

You will discover that your life is more joyful when you uproot your bitterness. If God gave us justice, every person reading this would die and go to hell. Thank God for His mercy that removes His hand of punishment from us. Praise God for His grace that gives us a brand-new life!

Bitterness is known in the Bible as spiritual poison and a means by which many are defiled (Hebrews 12:15). It is the source of countless spiritual and physical problems in millions of lives today. The Bible tells us that many are defiled using bitterness. Bitterness can be tricky to recognize, because it is not a symptom or visible on the surface like anger usually is. Many people claim they are not angry or hateful, but that's not what bitterness is all about. Bitterness is an underlying problem that does not always manifest outside but dwells in that person's system.

Bitterness is a deadly poison that needs to be brought into the light and addressed to bring people out of spiritual, emotional, and even physical bondage. Bitterness is a means for blasphemy, and countless sicknesses and diseases are a result of bitterness.

Desires, Quote from James 4, *Contemporary English Version* (CEV)

Why do you fight and argue with each other? Isn't it because you are full of selfish desires that want to control your body? You want something you do not have, and you will do anything to get it. You will even kill! But still you cannot get what you want, and you will not get it by fighting and arguing. You should pray for it. Yet even when you pray, your prayers are not answered because you pray just for selfish reasons.

You people aren't faithful to God! Don't you know if you love the world, you are God's enemies? If you decide to be a friend of the world, you make yourself an enemy of God. Do you doubt the Scriptures that say God genuinely cares about the Spirit he has put in you? God treats us with even more incredible kindness. God opposes everyone proud, but He blesses all who are humble with undeserved grace.

Surrender to God! Resist the devil, and he will run from you. Come near to God, and He will come near to you. Clean up your lives, you sinners. Purify your hearts, you people who cannot make up your mind. Be sad and sorry and weep. Stop laughing and start crying. Be gloomy instead of glad. Be humble in the Lord's presence, and He will honor you.

Try to live in peace with everyone! Live a clean life. If you do not, you will never see the Lord. Make sure no one misses out on God's incredible kindness. Do not let anyone become bitter and cause trouble for the rest of you. Do not love the world or anything that belongs to the world. If you love the world, you cannot love the Father. Our foolish pride comes from this world, and so do our selfish desires and our desire to have everything we see. None of this comes from the Father. The world and the desires it cause are disappearing. But if we obey God, we will live forever.

Stop being bitter and angry and mad at others. Do not yell at one another or curse each other or ever be rude. Instead, be kind and merciful, and forgive others, just as God forgave you because of Christ.

Sleep Balances Your Mind and Emotions. Research shows that a healthy sleep schedule has positive physical effects and can help temper emotional distress. Sleep, or the lack thereof, can influence emotions, mood, memory, decision-making, aggression, and more. Let us be clear on the role sleep plays in our lives. For starters, it is fundamental to our physical and mental wellbeing. Far from simply being a period of rest, sleep fosters muscle growth, repairs cells, and fortifies our immune system. It can help our heart and blood vessels repair themselves while our brains are busy sorting and filing memories and improving our learning ability the next day. But in times of stress and crisis, it can be a struggle to maintain a consistent sleep/wake routine.

And if you suffer from sleep apnea or long-term sleep deprivation, this has been linked to a smorgasbord of health disasters, including type 2 diabetes, heart disease, and cancer. Sleep affects how we process and store new memories and accurately retrieve old ones.

We are more likely to remember things that match our current mood. For example, if you are happy, pleasant memories are more forthcoming, whereas, in times of sadness or anger, less-pleasant memories emerge more quickly. The mood we are in can color how we perceive things that happen to us, how we interact with others, and the motivation to do things like exercise or work. Sleep-deprived people reported higher stress levels, anxiety, and anger on low-stress tasks than well-rested people. If our ability to regulate emotions and moods is affected by too little sleep, it stands to reason that we might be a little more on edge and prone to anger than usual when sleep deprived.

Studies on sleep and aggression found connections between sleep deprivation and increased anger, aggression, and short-tempered expression. Exact causes are difficult to identify, but research suggests this relationship may result from impaired prefrontal cortex functioning (responsible for control and regulation of emotions) and, for some individuals, variations in neurotransmitter and adrenal systems. Different aspects of cognition are involved in making decisions, and while mood and memory play essential roles, there is even more going on. This phenomenon is mainly due to reduced capacity for self-control. Other research suggests depleted glucose stores may affect frontal-lobe functioning required for complex thought and decision-making, increasing unethical actions. Sleeping and regularly waking, getting at least seven hours, getting regular exercise and good nutrition, and taking time to de-stress all help contribute to better rest.

If you find yourself facing an emotionally charged situation, sleep is even more critical. Clear your mind before bed with meditation or yoga, and then take the night to sleep on a tough decision and temper your thoughts.

Violence is the Norm, Not the Exception.

One cannot peruse man's history without reading about endless conflicts, tribal massacres, and nations at war. Century after century, nations and empires arise and then cease to exist, often with war providing both the source of their creation and the cause of their demise. The aftereffects linger for decades: hundreds of thousands of orphaned children, widowed women left homeless, crippled bodies of survivors, devastated infrastructure, and enduring economic ruin.

Waves of civil unrest, demonstrations, riots, and related chaos threaten governments in Egypt, Yemen, North Africa, Algeria, Tunisia, and the Ivory Coast. There are rumblings in Burma, Lebanon, Jordan, Iran, and China. Failure to prosecute criminals and militants for the violence they commit or instigate and distrust and growing dissatisfaction with weak or unpopular leaders all increase the potential for conflicts and uprisings in Colombia, Zimbabwe, Iraq, Venezuela, Sudan, Tajikistan, Haiti, and Guatemala. The Middle East is always a powder keg. Ours is a time of uncertainty, anxiety, and perplexity. War is now changing, becoming less conventional. It still results in death and destruction, but now it is labeled hybrid war. We are experiencing a fusion of war, terror, and crime. There are often no clear battle lines, no contested territories, and no identifiable differences between combatants and noncombatants. The enemy may be a stateless entity and live among the population in urban areas. The movement of the enemy may be on public thoroughfares or even public transportation systems. Targets may be innocent civilians in public places. World powers may use unrest and civil disturbances to carry out proxy war to pursue their interests in places where open war would be strategically unwise. Just as the apostle Paul wrote, the lesson of history is that mankind does not know the way to peace.

Surface Problem: Behavior

Surface Cause: Psychology

The Root of Bitterness: Theology

Three root problems: Bitterness, temporal values, moral impurity

Inner Conflicts (Notice the reverse order)

    8. Thoughts of suicide

    7. Depression

    6. Guilt

    5. Loneliness and insecurity

    4. Establish self as the authority

    3. Rejection of authority

2. Loss of love and respect

1. Hurt

Outer signs: available options

A. Attempt suicide

B. Bounce up and down the chart

C. Fixate on one place on the chart

D. Resolve root problem

Thrills and extremes:

A. Condemn others

B. Experiment with sin

C. Wrong friends of idols

D. Open rebellion

E. Stubbornness

F. Communication breakdown

How to Resolve a Root of Bitterness:

A. Admit there is a problem.

B. Decide to do something about it.

C. Ask God's help in the process.

D. Identify the source of the hurt (person or persons).

E. Decide to forgive.

F. Ask God's help

   1) to forgive and

   2) to know how to go about it.

G. Design an experience to be used as an emotional marker of a time, place, and statement (in prayer and in the presence of another person to look back on and say that is when and where I did it).

H. Begin to act and talk as though genuine forgiveness has occurred.

Your feelings will eventually come around.

Tearing Down the Strongholds of Bitterness
The soul is our minds, wills, and emotions vs. Spirit—
Hebrews 4:12.

The ground is the jurisdictional area (place in our souls)—
Ephesians 4:27.

Stronghold is a mindset and conclusion contrary to Scripture—
2 Corinthians 10:4–5.

Tormentors are afflictions allowed by God to teach us mercy—
Matthew 18:34.

A principality is a ruler of evil over a jurisdictional area—
Ephesians 6:12.

The heart is the door to the soul.

Our eyes are the door to the heart.

Fear, lust, anger, and bitterness are the seeds we plant in the surrendered ground.

I. Steps of Action:

A. Confess the sin of bitterness—Hebrews 12:15, 1 John 1:9.

B. Ask God to regain surrendered ground—Psalm 23:3.

C. Tear down strongholds with truth—2 Corinthians 10:4–5.

D. Show mercy by forgiving your offender—Matthew 6:14–15.

Session 9—Indwelling Sin

Indwelling sin hides in the human heart. Generally speaking, the heart in Scripture refers to the whole of the man considered as a moral being choosing evil or good. It has several faculties, including mind, emotions, will, and conscience. These were designed to function in a hierarchy of cooperative agreements, but not so since the Fall.

The heart in its deceitfulness and its unsearchableness increases the impact and power of indwelling sin upon us. Thus, we are commanded to never let up from mortification and to remain watchful for sin's uprising in the heart. Finally, we commit all these realities over to God, who knows our hearts thoroughly and can uncover sin for us. In this process, we are to follow the example of David in Psalm 139:23–24: "Examine me and probe my thoughts! Test me and know my concerns! See if there is any idolatrous tendency in me and lead me in the reliable ancient path!"

Realistic discussions about sin and its power in our lives could lead us to feelings of despair and anxiety if it were not for our Lord's gracious provision and presence. "Cast all your anxiety on Him because He cares for you" (1 Peter 5:7).

God can precisely search our hearts to the uttermost to know what lies beneath the surface, ready to undo us. He can make things known to us to protect and deliver us from the enemy. He knows the ways of our fallen hearts and is not the least bit fooled by them. He also loves us deeply, as the cross once-and-for-all teaches us. We need only follow the course set out for us by Israel's great king, David.

In contrast to a law imposed from the outside, indwelling sin is a law from within, and hence it has greater power to motivate, compel, and impel us into its service. It always abides in the soul; it is always ready to apply itself with rewards and punishments; it always affects the mind with darkness, the affections with sensuality, and the will with stubbornness. As Paul says, "When I would do good, sin is right there with me; it is ever-present."

In Scripture, the heart is the seat of indwelling sin as well as its subject. It is from the heart that indwelling sin springs in a person's experience. So says the preacher: "The unfortunate thing about everything that happens on earth, the same fate awaits everyone. The hearts of all people are full of evil, and there is madness in their hearts during their lives; then they die."

Matthew 15:18–20: "But the things that come out of the mouth come from the heart. These things defile a person. For out of the heart come evil ideas, murder, adultery, sexual immorality, theft, false testimony, slander. These are the things that defile a person; it is not eating with unwashed hands that defiles a person."

The problem we have comes from within us. From within that, our fallen, darkened hearts gush forth evil and corrupt the whole of our lives, seriously damaging the lives of those to whom we are most connected. In Genesis 6:5, the text pulls no punches, describing the depths to which the human heart can sink apart from God: "But the Lord saw that the wickedness of humankind had become great on the earth. Every inclination of the thoughts of their minds was only evil all the time. Out of the total population of the earth, only eight people were saved, and one of those eight was from Noah's family; his son Ham was evil. Ham had sex with his mother when Noah was drunk, and she became pregnant with Canaan. Therefore, Canaan's brothers were Japheth, Shem, and his brother Ham, who also, was his father; they all had the same mother." (See how Lev. 20:11 and Deut. 27:20 interpret the term "uncovered his father's nakedness" to mean that the son has committed adultery with his father's wife.) This sheds an entirely fresh light on Genesis 9:22, for it reveals that Ham's sin is not that he leered at Noah but that he had sex with Noah's wife, his own mother, while Noah was passed out

In contrast to Genesis 6–11, the believers are given a new heart, one that has righteousness as the roots of the thought-life, whose God-fearing thoughts produce the fruit of the Spirit. (See Galatians 5.) The good treasure of the believer's heart is none other than the indwelling of the Spirit of God.

Jesus said that the good person, out of his heart's good treasure, produces good, and the evil person, out of his evil treasure, produces evil (Luke 6:45). The fantastic treasure Jesus speaks of comes by grace, but evil treasure is the best man can produce apart from God's grace, in his pitiful, fallen state. These two treasures, ironically enough, do not run empty the more men draw upon them. Indeed, the more a person under God's grace draws on Christ's riches through faith and obedience, the more the principle of grace is strengthened in that person. On the other hand, the more a person feeds his sin through unbelief and disobedience, the more sin's power grows within, establishing a foothold and a fortress.

The more men exercise their grace in duties of obedience, the more it is strengthened and increased in them; and the more men exert and put forth the fruits of their lust, the more is that enraged and increased in them; it feeds upon itself, swallows up its poison, and grows thereby. The more men sin, the more they are inclined to sin. It is from the deceitfulness of this law of sin that men persuade themselves that by this or that particular sin they shall so satisfy their lusts as that they shall need to sin no more. Every sin increased the principle and fortified the habit of sinning, Psalm 40:12 "For evils beyond number have surrounded me; My iniquities have overtaken me, so that I am not able to see; They are more numerous than the hairs of my head, And my heart has failed me."

"There is no more realistic picture of the deceitfulness of sin than here presented. How many times have you heard people (myself/yourself) say: "I'll just do it this time and get it out of my system"? Nothing could be more deceitful than this. Do it once and you will do it twice is much closer to the truth. Our sinful lusts, which live and thrive in our hearts, gain ground through use, but they can be put to death (Romans 8:13).

"Thus, the Bible is everywhere realistic in its evaluation of the human heart. It recognizes the good from creation and God's grace but is utterly straightforward about the sin and folly bound up within us as well.

"Now concerning the heart as the principle of men's good or evil actions, two things may be said. First, there is a suitableness or pleasantness to the heart in what is done. Both God and men are said to do things wholeheartedly. Second, there is a resolution or constancy in the things that are done. Men's hearts continuously draw on the treasure within which they feel they need or intend to use. Thus, there is both a suitableness and a constancy in the workings of the heart.

"Much of the strength of indwelling sin, then, lies in this fact, namely, that the heart itself is beyond understanding; this allows sin to have its sway and power. Thus, we may suppose a particular sin to have been defeated when, in reality, it has only temporarily slipped out of sight where we cannot follow it and destroy it, only to reappear at a more convenient time.

"But Jeremiah's reference to the heart as deceitful is not connected with the deceitfulness of sin in society, as prevalent as that is. Instead, the prophet speaks of the deceitfulness in a man's heart toward himself.

"The frame of the heart is ready to contradict itself every moment."[42] Things can be going well, so to speak, with the mind, affections, and will at peace and operating correctly, but in the very next breath, the emotions can seize sovereignty, and all can descend in turmoil and contradictions. This is not how God created us, but it is the sad reality of our sin's impact.

"There is a second way, besides contradictions, that deceit operates in our hearts, by also making full promises at the first appearance of things. Sometimes our affections or emotions are touched upon, and all seems to be well with the heart. But our whole disposition or countenance is shaken within a short time, indicating that our mind had not also been touched or changed by God. Once the emotion is gone, all the fair promises we made regarding reform and holiness are gone with it; order of operations of the soul's faculties are dislodged by sin and thrown violently into confusion. We are not surprised that God warns us numerous times in Scripture to watch our hearts!

"If we were fighting against an enemy who presented himself in the open, that would be one thing; we could rest in peace knowing that he was far away at times or incapable of striking at others. But we wrestle not against such a foe. Sin living in the heart is deceitful, deals treacherously, and often comes by stealth. Therefore, we must be vigilant; we must watch and pray, as the Lord repeatedly taught us. Though the morning gives a fair appearance of serenity and peace, turbulent affections may arise and cloud the soul with sin and darkness."

Root Problems:

1. Root of bitterness

2. Temporal values

3. Moral impurity

Feeling hooks:

1. Habits

2. Compulsion

3. Obsessive compulsion

4. Addiction

Dr. Sydney: During our first two sessions, I learned a lot about you and your beliefs. Now what I am looking for are feelings attached to your thoughts. These are examples I want you to follow:

How did you feel when your mother told you that you couldn't sit in her lap any longer when your baby sister was born?

How did you feel when your grandpa told your dad that you would never amount to anything?

How did you feel when your mother said you were lying when you said you were sick?

How did you feel when your sister told you to light the firecracker in the fresh cow dung?

How did you feel when your daddy used the razor strap to whip you and continued whipping you until you cried, and then you immediately had to stop when he said that was enough crying?

Your statements should start with "I felt ___" (fill in the blank), like the examples from the following chart.

Please do as many as you can think of using this format. I want to review these in two weeks. You can use a computer or paper, whichever you prefer.

1. Leave enough space between each statement so you can cut them out.

2. Sort them into patterns or themes.

3. After they are sorted, either glue or tape each under the appropriate theme.

Jerry, this exercise I am asking you to do is not to blame anyone or cause you shame. You are a son of God, and as such, He has already forgiven you of all sin and no longer sees any of them because they are under the blood of Jesus, who has washed away your guilt and shame. Unless you share these details with someone, they are for you and me. Please be as honest as you can, for the most profound healing will only come as you uncover and expose them to God. He already knows, and He wants you to acknowledge them to Him. He loves and accepts you. Some things may not come to memory, as they are so profoundly suppressed. It may be years before you need to deal with them, using this same approach you are learning now.

You have the rest of the session to begin your list. You will need six or seven sheets of paper. On each page, put the appropriate timeframe, then follow this chart for details.

How to Determine the Truth/The Top Ten Misbelief Breakers

1. On what facts or logical argument do I base this notion?

2. What is the most compelling evidence I can produce to contest this notion?

3. What is the worst thing that could happen? What if it did happen? Is it likely to be as dreadful as it appears to me now?

4. What are the more profound misbeliefs that underlie my painful thoughts?

5. Have I found verses to support my negative thoughts and beliefs? What are they? Do they apply to this situation?

6. Have I found written material that disputes this thought? What is it? If the writings disagree with Scripture and me, does God's Word on the subject settle it? If not, can I continue to tell myself this misbelief?

7. What could I do to curb or change this notion if it causes me trouble? Are these painful, automatic thoughts based on truth or are they merely information I thought were correct but are false?

8. Is this something I do automatically, or is it merely a bad habit?

9. Could the effects of this situation be explained in other ways? Are there alternative interpretations I could give things that would be less painful and more truthful? What are they?

10. Is it all my fault? Am I totally to blame? Is there anything to be gained from deciding who is to blame?

Forgiveness is more about you than them. When you do not forgive, the bitterness you have against that person will take root in you and rob you of a close relationship with God. Eventually, you will become the person you hate in them, and you sure do not want to be like them in any shape or form. The emotions you have toward the offender will cause you to be a bitter person. Dr. Gilliam used the illustration of you drinking rat poison and waiting for the other person to die. God will not answer your prayer when you are holding a grudge.

"For if you forgive others for their transgressions, your heavenly Father will also forgive you. But if you do not forgive others, then your Father will not forgive your transgressions" (Matthew 6:14).

Rethink your position on forgiveness. You want to get to the point that you can hold your head high. God tells us that He does not condemn those in Christ Jesus who walk not after the flesh but after the Spirit. You forgive anyone who caused the hurt, and then let the pain go, in Jesus's name.

You may think "I cannot," but with God's help, you can. Let God's Word continue to mold and mature your life. Let God place in your heart the fruit of the Spirit: love, joy, peace, patience, kindness, goodness, faithfulness, gentleness, and self-control. Press forward by walking in the Spirit. When you are confronted by people who can hurt you with their words or actions, you can tell that person to stop. If they continue, walk away. Focus on Christ, not the circumstances that lead to the hurt, and He will help you recover from the pains in life.

Jesus freed you from all strongholds. Remind yourself that you are complete in Jesus and do not need to feel inferior. You are all right the way God made you, and He sees you as His adopted son who lacks nothing. You are loved and forgiven in God's eyes.

PERSONAL JOURNEY CHART – CHRONOLOGICAL HISTORY OF ABUSE

Compose a chart of your personal journey from earliest years to present using these timeframes (as appropriate).

Timeframe Baby, Toddler, preschool, adolencent, teenager, young adult, adult

Time Frame	People Involved	What Happened	What Emotions You Felt	Your Interpretation of Why This Happened	What You Promised Yourself to Protect Yourself

"Put Off... Put On"

"That ye put off concerning the former conversation the old man, which is corrupt according to the deceitful lusts." Ephesians 4:22

"But put ye on the Lord Jesus Christ, and make not provision for the flesh, to fulfil the lusts thereof." Romans 13:14

"Put Off"	Scriptural Insight	"Put On"
1. Lack of love	*I John 4:7,8,20* · *John 15:12*	Love
2. Judging	*Matthew 7:1,2* · *John 8:9;15:22*	Let God search my heart
3. Bitterness	*Hebrews 12:15* · *Ephesians 4:32*	Tender hearted and forgiving
4. Unforgiving spirit	*Mark 11:26* · *Colossians 3:13*	Forgiving spirit
5. Selfishness	*Philippians 2:21* · *John 12:24*	Self denial
6. Pride	*Proverbs 16:5* · *James 4:6*	Humility
7. Boasting (conceit)	*I Corinthians 4:7* · *Philippians 2:3*	Esteeming others
8. Stubbornness	*I Samuel 15:23* · *Romans 6:13*	Brokenness
9. Disrespect for authority	*Acts 23:5* · *Hebrews 13:17*	Honor authority
10. Rebellion	*I Samuel 15:23* · *Hebrews 13:17*	Submission
11. Disobedience	*I Samuel 12:15* · *Deuteronomy 11:27*	Obedience
12. Impatience	*James 1:2-4* · *Hebrews 10:36*	Patience
13. Ungratefulness	*Romans 1:21* · *Ephesians 5:20*	Gratefulness
14. Covetousness	*Luke 12:15* · *Hebrews 13:5*	Contentment
15. Discontent	*Hebrews 13:5* · *I Timothy 6:8*	Contentment
16. Murmuring/complaining	*Philippians 2:14* · *Hebrews 13:15*	Praise
17. Irritation to others	*Galatians 5:26* · *Philippians 2:3,4*	Preferring in love
18. Jealousy	*Galatians 5:26* · *I Corinthians 13:4*	Trust
19. Strife/contention	*Proverbs 13:10* · *James 3:17*	Peace
20. Retaliation (getting even)	*Proverbs 24:29* · *Romans 12:19,20*	Return good for evil
21. Losing temper	*Proverbs 25:28* · *Proverbs 16:32*	Self-control
22. Anger	*Proverbs 29:22* · *Galatians 5:22,23*	Self-control
23. Wrath	*James 1:19,20* · *Proverbs 15:1*	Soft answer
24. Easily irritated	*I Corinthians 13:5* · *Proverbs 19:11*	Not easily provoked
25. Hatred	*Matthew 5:21,22* · *I Corinthians 13:3*	Love
26. Murder	*Exodus 20:13* · *Romans 13:10*	Love
27. Gossip	*I Timothy 5:13* · *Ephesians 4:29*	Edifying speech
28. Evil speaking	*James 4:11* · *Proverbs 15:30*	Good report
29. Critical spirit	*Galatians 5:15* · *Colossians 3:12*	Kindness
30. Lying	*Ephesians 4:25* · *Zechariah 8:16*	Speak truth
31. Profanity	*Proverbs 4:24* · *Proverbs 15:4*	Pure speech
32. Idle words	*Matthew 12:36* · *Proverbs 21:23*	Bridle tongue
33. Wrong motives	*I Samuel 16:7* · *I Corinthians 10:31*	Spiritual motives
34. Evil thoughts	*Matthew 15:19-20* · *Philippians 4:8*	Pure thoughts
35. Complacency	*Revelation 3:15* · *Revelation 3:19*	Zeal
36. Laziness	*Proverbs 20:4* · *Proverbs 6:6-11*	Diligence
37. Slothfulness (not doing best)	*Proverbs 18:9* · *Colossians 3:23*	Wholeheartedness

"Put Off"	*Scriptural Insight*	*"Put On"*
38. Hypocrisy .... *Job 8:13*	*I Thessalonians 2:3* .... Sincerity
39. Idolatry .... *Deuteronomy 11:16*	*Colossians 1:18* .... Worship God only
40. Left first love .... *Revelation 2:4*	*Revelation 2:5* .... Fervent devotion
41. Lack of rejoicing always .... *Philippians 4:4*	*I Thessalonians 5:18* .... Rejoice
42. Worry/fear .... *Matthew 6:25-32*	*I Peter 5:7* .... Trust
43. Unbelief .... *Hebrews 3:12*	*Hebrews 11:1,6* .... Faith
44. Unfaithfulness .... *Proverbs 25:19*	*Luke 16:10-12* .... Faithfulness
45. Neglect of Bible study .... *II Timothy 3:14-17*	*Psalm 1:2* .... Bible study/meditation
46. Prayerlessness .... *Luke 18:1*	*Matthew 26:41* .... Praying
47. No burden for the lost .... *Matthew 9:36-38*	*Acts 1:8* .... Compassion/witnessing
48. Burying talents .... *Luke 12:48*	*I Corinthians 4:2* .... Developing abilities
49. Irresponsibility (family/work) ...... *Luke 16:12*	*Luke 16:10* .... Responsibility
50. Procrastination .... *Proverbs 10:5*	*Proverbs 27:1* .... Diligence
51. Irreverence in church .... *Ecclesiastes 5:1*	*Psalm 89:7* .... Reverence
52. Inhospitable .... *I Peter 4:9*	*Romans 12:13* .... Hospitable
53. Cheating .... *II Corinthians 4:2*	*II Corinthians 8:21* .... Honesty
54. Stealing .... *Proverbs 29:24*	*Ephesians 4:28* .... Working/giving
55. Lack of moderation .... *Proverbs 11:1*	*I Corinthians 9:25* .... Temperance
56. Gluttony .... *Proverbs 23:21*	*I Corinthians 9:27* .... Discipline
57. Wrong friends .... *Psalm 1:1*	*Proverbs 13:20* .... Godly friends
58. Temporal values .... *Matthew 6:19-21*	*II Corinthians 4:18* .... Eternal values
59. Love of money/greed .... *I Timothy 6:9,10*	*Matthew 6:33* .... Love God
60. Stinginess .... *I John 3:17*	*Proverbs 11:24,25* .... Generosity
61. Moral impurity .... *I Thessalonians 4:7*	*I Thessalonians 4:4* .... Moral purity
62. Fornication .... *I Corinthians 6:18*	*I Thessalonians 4:3* .... Abstinence
63. Lust .... *I Peter 2:11*	*Titus 2:12* .... Pure desires
64. Adultery .... *Matthew 5:27,28*	*Proverbs 5:14-19* .... Marital fidelity
65. Homosexuality .... *Leviticus 18:22*	*I Thessalonians 4:4,5* .... Moral purity
66. Incest .... *Leviticus 18:6*	*I Corinthians 7:2,5* .... Moral purity
67. Pornography .... *Psalm 101:3*	*Philippians 4:8* .... Pure thoughts
68. Immodest dress .... *Proverbs 7:10*	*I Timothy 2:9* .... Modesty
69. Flirtation .... *Proverbs 7:21*	*I Peter 3:4* .... Gentle, quiet spirit
70. Worldly entertainment .... *Proverbs 21:17*	*Galatians 5:16* .... Spiritual pursuits
71. Fleshly music .... *Ephesians 4:29,30*	*Ephesians 5:19* .... Edifying music
72. Bodily harm .... *I Corinthians 3:16,17*	*I Corinthians 6:19,20* .... Glorify God in body
73. Alcoholism .... *Proverbs 20:1*	*Proverbs 23:30* .... Abstinence
74. Following the crowd .... *Proverbs 1:10*	*Proverbs 3:7* .... God-fearing
75. Witchcraft/astrology/ horoscopes .... *Deuteronomy 18:10,11*	*Deuteronomy 6:5* .... Worship of God
76. Gambling .... *Proverbs 28:20,22*	*Luke 16:11* .... Good Stewardship
77. Preferential treatment .... *James 2:1-9*	*Luke 6:31* .... Love neighbor as self
78. Presumption on the future .... *Proverbs 27:1*	*James 4:14-16* .... Trust God's will

"But there is forgiveness with Thee . . ." Psalm 130:4

Column One Your False Belief is a Lie	Column Two Correct it with God Says[77]	Column Three Scripture is Truth
You say I cannot figure it out.	God says I will direct your step, Prov. 3:5-6	
You say I am too tired.	God says I will give your rest, Matt. 11:28–30	
You say it is impossible.	God says all things are possible, Luke 18:27	
You say nobody loves me.	God says I love you, John 3:16	
You say I cannot forgive myself.	God says I forgive you, Romans 8:1	
You say it is not worth it.	God says it will be worth it, Romans 8:28	
You say I am not smart enough.	God says I will give you wisdom, 1 Cor. 1:30	
You say I am not able.	God says I am capable, 2 Cor. 9:8	
You say I cannot go on.	God speaks my grace is sufficient, 2 Cor.12:0	
You say I cannot manage.	God says I will supply all your needs, Phil. 4:119	
You say I cannot do it.	God says you can do all things, Phil..4:13	
You say I am afraid.	God says I have not given you fear, 2 Tim. 1:7	
You say I feel all alone.	God says I will never leave you, Hebrews 13:5	

Your belief system is the backbone of our work together. Identifying your beliefs is an essential part of all our counseling sessions. I want you to identify your beliefs and be prepared for the vast change coming to your life.

Once we have identified your belief system, we will correct the false beliefs we found and compare them with Scripture. That is when the "Put On—Put Off" charts will help you.

JERRY: I started a list, but I'm not sure this is what you wanted me to do.

1. When I was about five years old, my cousin, aged ten, told me he had a new game to play We were in the barn, and he took off all his clothes and sat on the edge of the cattle-loading ramp. I was standing on the ground in front of him, and my head was just eye level with the ramp. He asked me to give him oral sex. He said it was a game only he and I would play, and it was a secret. I promised not to tell anyone.

    I liked doing it. I had never seen another penis before. I felt special. I didn't realize doing this with him would later become a problem for me. He was the only boy I played with until the fifth grade.

2. I was preadolescent at the start of fifth grade. I was timid, immature, and was a loner. I was naïve about many things. I had forgotten (blocked) my childhood memories of sexual abuse. I did not know what a gay person was. I heard the dirty talk, not realizing how boys thought about girls and each other. I thought of girls as I did my sisters, someone you treated with respect and I thought oral sex was something all boys did with each other.

    At recess, several boys from class caught me and dragged me over to where the girls were and pulled down my pants, leaving me half-naked in from them. I was humiliated and horrified. They ran away laughing, but I just wanted to die with embarrassment. I never wanted anyone to see my penis, especially girls. This happened at least once a week. They also beat me and called me dirty names.

3. During recess, the boys were bragging about the size of their penises. Two boys took theirs out to show. A boy named Pet Odom

had the biggest one. It was the second hard penis I had ever seen in my life, and it was a whopper.

4. After seeing him, I ran away, but the memory of my secret game came back loud and clear, and I didn't know what to do with my feelings. I pretended I was playing the secret game, not with my cousin, but with Pet. I wanted to act this out with Pet, but I could not trust him to keep it a secret. I avoided Pet as much as possible after that. I was afraid someone might read my mind and find out what I was really like on the inside.

The next year I became a Christian, but I still maintained an active, dirty thought-life. I had no Christian men to say to me, "Jerry, have you asked Jesus to clean up your dirty thought-life? This is how you should think about girls. If you thought of that girl as a sister you were close to, would you still want to have sex with her? If she were your sister and somebody you didn't care for was trying to get her to have sex with him, would you protect her? Treat all girls as potential marriage material. You wouldn't want to marry someone if you knew she was sleeping around with anyone who dated her. Respect and honor girls, because they do not want to marry a person who has his penis in every girl he dates."

By the time I was in the military, I was ashamed and embarrassed by my thoughts, and I didn't know what to do about the raging sex drive I had. Then I met the Navigators.[43] These people were like nobody I had ever met before. They lived what they believed. Through Bible study, they helped me understand what being a Christian meant and how God expected His followers to be holy in their thoughts and behavior. The Navigators were the first men who shared how an unmarried Christian man was to behave with an unmarried Christian woman.

Dr. Sydney: Jerry, are ready to let God have those shameful images and thoughts? God loves you too much to let you stay stuck in those old ruts of thinking and acting. You have to be willing for God to work within you. You are safe here. Do you want to stay stuck or move on to newness of life?

Jerry: I am ready for God to work. God, I give you permission to work in whatever way You need in my life. I want my life to please you. Amen.

Jerry: It is time for us to take a careful look at the internal speech you have with yourself. When we know what you secretly think about, we can over-write the negative stuff and program positive edifying secret talk for you to tape over those old unwanted messages. This is the start of identifying your belief system. I will guide you step by step how to do this.

We will identify as many of the negative thoughts that you can think of.

Jerry, I want you to stop and calm your thoughts, take several deep breaths. Now let your thoughts come. Write them down as fast as you can for several minutes. After a couple of minutes, stop and read what you have written down. Now track your thought for five minutes. Did you notice a pattern?

The way you are talking to yourself directly influences every aspect of your life. We can be our own worst enemy at times and our internal conversation and negative thoughts can be extremely limiting. Were you blind to how negative your self-talk is to yourself?

How much of your negative thoughts were facts? They were not facts at all, but instead self-imposed limitations that you were putting on yourself. You also have the power to remove them. We will learn how to do that a little later. Would you be surprised to know that most people actually have remarkably similar negative thoughts? Here are some of the most common negative thoughts we all have and what we should think instead.

1. I Am Not Good Enough.

We tend to drown in this emotion of self-doubt and pity. It can be a symptom of low self-esteem, but the truth is that every one is good enough. Kirstin O'Donovan, Negative Thoughts We All Have and What to Think Instead,[44] used the illustration of a ten-dollar bill. Suppose you drop that $10 into a mud puddle, does that $10 lose it value. Of course not! We don't loose value just because of what we have done.[45] She gives us positive things to replace those negative ones. I recommend her excellent article.

The most important person in the universe has this to say about the value of a single person.

"While we were sinners—So far from being good, that we were not even just.[46] But God commended his love. His love is not like human love. Christ died, not for friends, but for enemies. It was "while we were yet sinners" that he died for us. Romans 5:8 But God demonstrates His own love toward us, in that while we were still sinners, Christ died for us."[47] This is huge!

2. I Can't Do It.

These four words "I can't do it" must be eradicated from your thinking beginning NOW. While you at it, get rid of it's companions as well—"But; Always and Never; Should, Would, Could; Have to Need to, Must!" These self-limiting words hold you back from being all you can be.

Your mind won't try if you have already told it that something is impossible.

Instead of focusing your negative thoughts on what you think you can't do, tell yourself, "I can do whatever I put my mind to." While we all do have limitations, believing in your abilities is the first step to achieving your short- and long-term goals in life.

3. I'm Not as Lucky as Other People

It is an illusion that other people's lives are better or luckier than yours. Use a sense of gratitude to begin to notice all of the good things you would normally never notice. For example, when was the last time you felt grateful for the roof over your head, the food in your fridge, or your comfy bed?

What would it be like if you believed that you could do what you really desired and have the experiences you wished instead? It is not about getting it right the first time but trying. Don't stop yourself before you have even given yourself a chance.

Don't limit yourself, instead, tell yourself, "I am confident I will…" Even if you don't feel confident in this moment, feeding your brain positive thoughts will slowly build.

Tell yourself, "I am making an effort to change what I don't like." Everyone has parts of themselves that they hope to improve, and this is certainly possible, but it requires approaching these things with a sense of self-love and patience.

Set yourself goals for the things you are not happy with instead of telling yourself what you "should" be like or be doing. Act the things you wish to change and remove limiting modals from your vocabulary.

Some Ways to Improve Yourself

The most important conversation you have with yourself is tell yourself that you are strong enough to deal with the challenges in front of you and support yourself in finding the strength you need in that moment. Do your best to cultivate those relationships and accept the love others are willing to give in order to combat your negative thoughts. Instead of believing that you're not intelligent, remind yourself that you are smart in a unique way and that you are capable of improving your knowledge in any area you choose. Lifelong learning can be a goal you constantly work toward. When facing a challenging situation or possible risk, tell yourself, "I am going to try; I am not scared of failing; that is not what is important." Even if you "fail," you will learn something about the world and yourself, and as long as that's the case, nothing is ever a true failure.

What would it be like if you imagined the best-case scenario? Our positive thoughts are very powerful, and it's common to use visualization as a technique to imagine the best-case scenario.

Think of the best that will happen when you try something new.

We all have negative thoughts from time to time. However, when the majority of your thoughts are negative, you are undermining your happiness at the end of the day. Our thoughts directly affect how we feel and, therefore, what we do in life. Don't limit yourself or what is possible for you. Master your thoughts and change your results. Remember everything that's part of your life was attracted by you, good and bad. Maybe you were conscious about it, but most likely is that you weren't. From now on, you have to start to create your future life in a conscious way.

SESSION 10—OUR BELIEFS

We will look at the lies you identified and the truths that counter them, starting with "I wasn't safe being me, so I pretended I was someone else."

JERRY: As a child, I couldn't isolate myself from my abusers, because they were family. I wanted to get away from them but had to live with them. Emotionally and physically, I was stuck. I chose to pretend I was someone else, safe, and far away. I trained myself to be in a distant place, and from there watched the horrible things done to me without any feeling. Feelings were scary. Besides, when I shared my feelings, others overruled me. I believed what they told me. I lived a very lonely life. Being someone else was always better than being me.

Now, as an adult, I will see if you are trustworthy. God uses people to minister to people. I will trust you to demonstrate God's character to me.

"Therefore, humble yourselves under the mighty hand of God, so that He may exalt you at the proper time, having cast all your anxiety on Him because He cares about you" (1 Peter 5:6–7).

Dr. Sydney: Now this one: "I shut down my emotions, so I don't have to deal with the pain from the abuser."

Jerry: I longed for tender touch when it happened but received pain, so I shut down my emotions. At school, I did not know how to play sports and was always the last one to be on a team. I rarely received compliments from friends, teachers, or family. I received many negative comments. Even as an adult, I received few compliments for something I did. I hungered for my parents to tell me they loved me, but I don't remember them ever saying those words. When my sister and I got into trouble, Mother made us kiss each other and say we were sorry. I hated kissing my sister.

As I grew older, an embrace often led to sexual activity. I startle easily, and certain people used this to harass me, then laughed when I jumped. They would catch me by surprise, put their hands on my shoulders, and after I settled down, would give me a back rub. I learned to hate hugs or back rubs.

I was so bruised by sexual abuse I sealed off all sexual feeling as if it were atomic waste and buried it so deep that no one will ever cause me pain again. I rather go without sex all my life than hurt like that again. Even masturbation lost it appeal and did not mean anything. Later, the sex act was just a way of self-punishment for me to beat myself up for being human with a sex drive. It did not feel pleasure, but searing pain of pealing the skin off the head.

I am all right and not damaged goods. I have value as a person. I can accept compliments and gentle touches without fear. I am strong enough to set appropriate boundaries when others act in an unhealthy way to me. I am okay with hugs at church.

I know this is out of context and refers to King Cyrus, but I believe God could say something like this to me: "I will go before you and make the rough places smooth; I will shatter the doors of bronze and cut through their iron bars. I will give you the treasures of darkness and hidden wealth of secret places, so that you may know that it is I, the LORD, the God of Israel, who calls you by your name. For the sake of Jacob, My servant, and Israel, My chosen one, I have also called you by your name; I have given you a title of honor" (Isaiah 45:2–4).

DR. SYDNEY: The lie: "I will be punished for sharing my emotions."

JERRY: As a child, I received punishment for saying to my abusive sister that I hated her. I was told people never knew someone as emotionally closed as I was.

As an adult, I had six years of weekly intense therapy, attended about eight workshops on relating to others, went to seminary and trained as a counselor, and attended more workshops. Still, I was not emotionally healthy where I could freely share my feelings with others. I had over eight years in GriefShare and Stephen's Ministry as a co-leader. Over those eight years, l helped others deal with their emotions, which, in turn, helped me share my feelings. I would not be the person I am today without all that baggage and the recovery involved in ministering to others.

It is okay to have feelings.

"Bless those who persecute you; bless and do not curse. Rejoice with those who rejoice, and weep with those who weep. Agree toward one another; do not be haughty in mind, but associate with the lowly. Do not be wise in your estimation. Never repay evil for evil to anyone. Respect what is right in the sight of all people. If possible, so far as it depends on you, be at peace with all people. Never take your revenge, beloved, but leave room for the wrath of God, for it is written: 'Vengeance is Mine, I will repay,' says the Lord. But if your enemy is hungry, feed him; if he is thirsty, give him a drink; for in so doing, you will heap burning coals on his head. Do not be overcome by evil but overcome evil with good" (Romans 12:14–21).

DR. SYDNEY: The lie: "No one believes what I say, and my opinions don't matter when I express them."

Jerry: I did not usually tell lies. No one believed my pain was real or cared about my feelings. As far back as I can remember, I often had migraines with an upset stomach. Mother took my temperature, and if it was as expected, she told me it was all in my head and to get over it. She said it was not real and that I was looking for an excuse to get out of school. So I'd go to school, and the teacher didn't believe me when I said I didn't feel well. But one occasion stands out in my memory. I requested my second toilet break, and the teacher refused me. I stood up and ran but only got to the end of the row when I vomited all over the floor. The teacher then let me sit outside in the fresh air. After that, when I raised my hand to go to the toilet, there was no problem. I trained her.

In hindsight, most of my headaches were from others acting out sexually with me. I received cold sores on my chin, and this I linked to the problems and abuse.

"In all their affliction, he was afflicted, and the angel of his presence saved them; in his love and his pity, he redeemed them; he lifted them and carried them all the days of old" (Isaiah 63:9).

Dr. Sydney: The lie: "My task in life is either sink or swim. I cannot trust those with me for help."

Jerry: I learned to be resourceful. Mother let me play near the pool and catch crawdads, minnows, and frogs. If I was not there, I played with the dogs or cats. Otherwise, I only had my family to play with, not friends.

I can get more satisfaction from trusting a person and believing in the 50 percent good in them than worrying about the damage their 50 percent wrong will do me, when I do not know which way it will be. I can also choose to harm them or do them good. God cares enough about me to mature and equip me for life in relationships. He uses people to do that.

"Therefore, encourage one another and build up one another, just as you also are doing" (1 Thessalonians 5:11).

Dr. Sydney: The lie: "I have been so wounded in relationships that I can only trust God, and sometimes myself."

Jerry: I was always unsure of myself. I could not choose the shirt I wanted to buy, what I wanted to eat, or where I wanted to go. I went along with the crowd.

I do not understand it, but somehow God is making me a different person than I was before. Instead of wanting to run away from others, I now desire to comfort those who are hurting. I can believe in others for the good that I find in them.

"Do not fear! These are the things which you shall do: Speak the truth to one another; judge with truth and judgment for peace at your gates" (Zechariah 8:15–16).

Dr. Sydney: The lie: "I wear what others put on me, the label."

Jerry: I believed whatever people told me I was. In school, classmates called me a sissy or Mommy's boy. I was naive regarding the real purpose and meaning of sex. I learned "sex" was a dirty word that caused me spankings, even though I didn't know why.

I can be myself. Let people respond how they desire. Pretending hinders others from getting close to me and me to others.

"My son, if sinners entice you, do not consent" (Proverbs 1:10).

Dr. Sydney: The lie: "Nothing is lasting and stable. I do not belong and connect."

Jerry: I never made a friend quickly, but when I did, he and I were inseparable. I had few friends until I entered the USAF and Bible college. My life changed drastically, and I became confident knowing I did things well.

My soul's anchor and my security are Jesus. He will never leave me or forsake me. He cares enough to love me through others.

"Treat people the same way you want them to treat you" (Luke 6:31).

Dr. Sydney: The lie: "I am a square peg in a round hole. I do not fit anywhere."

Jerry: Only God knows whether I am a square peg or a round hole. I might be a triangle or rectangle. God knows where I fit in His plan, and I need not worry. He opens doors and He closes doors. I will trust Him for guidance, whether to pick one or the other. I only know I can stake my life on God. I willingly imagine my future to Him one moment, one day, one week, one month, and one year at a time.

God made the peg, and He made the hole. He made me and knew where I fit best. Either God changes me or the hole. When I am responsive to Him, He takes the rough edges off, and I fit fine when He puts me in the hole. If the hole is round, He made me round. If the hole is square, He made me square. Whichever way, I fit fine and am secure and useful.

"'Can I not, O house of Israel, deal with you as this potter does?' declares the Lord. 'Behold, like the clay in the potter's hand, so are you in my hand, O house of Israel. At one moment, I might speak concerning a nation or concerning a kingdom to uproot, to pull down, or to destroy it'" (Jeremiah 18:6–7).

Dr. Sydney: The lie: "I deserve all the trouble I have."

Jerry: Do I deserve the trouble I have? If I have broken the law, I could be in trouble with the court that chooses whether I am innocent or guilty. When I have done no wrong and someone accuses me of doing such and such, my conscience clears or condemns me. I rest my case in God's hands and know He forgives me for the wrong I have done, whether to a person or against Him. Trouble is not my middle name, and I am not your doormat. I am I, and I am proud to be me. I am precious and loved.[48]

"'For I know the plans that I have for you,' declares the LORD, 'plans for prosperity and not for disaster, to give you a future and a hope'" (Jeremiah 29:11).

Dr. Sydney: The lie: "I cannot please significant others."

Jerry: I tried pleasing others, and that nearly killed me. God said that each day has enough of its problems and for us not to borrow for tomorrow. We only have today. Why should I spend my time and energy pleasing others when they do not care for themselves? My allegiance is for God and not for all my needy friends.

It is easy to use someone for your gain and not compensate your friend for what you did for him. In Stephen's Ministry, I learned to say no to a person who wanted me to do something for them when they had others in their circle of relations to do that. Giving in and violating this principle we called "Feeding the cat."[49] Many may say "I do not want to bother my children, so please do this for me."

Wow! Red flags are waving directly at you: no feeding the cat, meaning being too involved with your care receiver's life, enabling them, and doing for them what family or friends should be handling.

"One who is gracious to a poor person lends to the Lord, and He will repay him for his good deed" (Proverbs 10:17).

Dr. Sydney: The lie: "If I can get away, I can be free. Significant others will try to hold me back."

Jerry: I thought if I could only leave my family, I would be free. I joined the U.S. Air Force just after high school for this very reason. That is why I went to New Guinea. That is why I lived in Washington State. The subconscious communicates with our body and brain to do certain things, and we don't even realize we are following a script recorded from childhood on how we should feel and act. We can never run away from our past. Until it's reconciled, the past will catch up with us in the future.

Where can I go to be free? I cannot get away from myself. Where could I go but to the Lord?

"Do not boast about tomorrow, for you do not know what a day may bring" (Proverbs 27:1).

Dr. Sydney: The lie: "My ideas do not count."

Jerry: My ideas count, and I can share them when appropriate to others and not feel guilty about betraying myself. The irrational promises a child makes have no fulfillment. When I realize the folly of this, I have the responsibility to myself to change those beliefs into truths that I intend to keep, with God's help. I am talented and have promising ideas.

I have all my needs met by God, according to his glorious riches in Christ Jesus, according to Philippians 4:19.

"For our exhortation does not come from error or impurity or by way of deceit; but just as we have been approved by God to be entrusted with the Gospel, so we speak, not intending to please people, but to please God, who examines our hearts" (1 Thessalonians 4:3–4).

Dr. Sydney: The lie: "Life is empty; I must medicate to survive."

Jerry: I received Jesus as my Savior in 1956. Only He is the true one to fill my life. Dabbling in witchcraft and using drugs for mind control will only leave the person in slavery. That is not the answer. The Bible tells us to flee temptation that corrupts our bodies with something that is physically hurtful and usually leads to that person's death by overdose. Instead, change life to full by getting rid of the void causing the desire for medication.

"Therefore, let the one who thinks he stands, watch out that he does not fall. No temptation has overtaken you except something common to humankind. God is faithful. He will not allow you to be tempted beyond what you are able but will provide the way of escape also so that you will be able to endure it" (1 Corinthians 10:12–13).

Dr. Sydney: The lie: "Boys do not have equal rights with girls."

Jerry: Being surrounded by females, I had male deference. My family had strong women who made the decisions. I had no male role models. Women bossed everything while the men made money. Back then, women kept the home, raised the children, and worked in the fields.   Women, strong ones, did everything around the house. My dad worked from sunrise to sunset, and my mother made the decisions. I grew up thinking girls were strong and got things done.

When we moved to West Texas, I found out from the boys in the local gang that boys and men are stronger and dangerous to be around. These boys harassed me on the playground and after school. They criticized me regularly and sexually abused me.

I am as much a person as any other, male, or female. I am a whole person, not half of a person. Male and female both reflect the character of God.

"Do you not know you are a temple of God and that the Spirit of God dwells in you? If anyone destroys the temple of God, God will destroy that person; the temple of God is holy, and that is what you are" (1 Corinthians 3:16–17).

Dr. Sydney: The lie: "Because of abuse as a child, I must be fundamentally flawed and have no value."

Jerry: Because I am a child of God, I trust my heavenly Father to pull me out of the past's terrible memories and instill values in me with a sound understanding of His love, affection, and touch. I purpose to receive my heavenly Father's love and comfort, which will make me whole, so I will value myself as God does.

I learned that by saying I will do this or that, something happens to prevent me from doing just that. The issues I thought finished show up later to be redone.

The fundamental truth is, with all the tradition that holds my world together removed, I am face-to-face with God, and God makes no sense to me. I believe my question must be, "What do I do with God?" Do I reject Him, or do I fall on my knees and say, "I need your help; I do want to trust you!"

When people belittled me repeatedly, I began to believe those were my thoughts. Mostly they were inaccurate descriptions and had no truth in them, but I could not discern the difference. I accepted what others told me, and if I disagreed, I was overruled and told I couldn't make the right decisions for myself.

I stuffed everything about my abuse, including my feelings, the violence, and my fears. It was a miracle Jerry Wayne survived. Dr. Sydney, you told me God does not make junk. Being of no value was so ingrained in me from early childhood that I believed it to be true. But eventually I learned to recognize what was true and what was false. I had no standard to guide me. Only through demanding work with my therapist did I learn God loved me. But I had a problem. In 1 John 2, God states if you say you love Him and hate your neighbor, you are calling God a liar. How could I love my neighbor and not love myself? I hated myself. It was a long, challenging, and painful soul-searching process. I had to fully embrace God and those I could trust, and then gain confidence in myself.

"By this we know that we have come to know Him if we keep His commandments. The one who says, 'I have come to know Him' and does not keep His commandments is a liar, and the truth is not in him; but whoever follows His Word, in him the love of God has truly been perfected. By this, we know that we are in Him: the one who says that he remains in Him ought, himself also, walk just as He walked" (1 John 2:3–6).

DR. SYDNEY: The lie: "My life stinks and is not worth living; my life sentence is a total, permanent rip-off."

JERRY: The Holy Spirit will hover over the chaos and darkness of my life so that Jesus can speak beauty into it. My life is not a mistake and not a total, permanent rip-off. Jesus did not create chaos or trash. God forgives me for the poor choices I have made. He is healing the trauma and damage done to me by others. He is giving me a future with faith, hope, and love.

I want to enjoy life to the fullest, starting today. I claim freedom from the baggage of the past that robbed me of the joy of living. With a healthy fear of God and using appropriate boundaries, I choose to be spontaneous, passionate, vulnerable, and joy-filled in experiencing the abundant life promised me. When I think of happiness, I respond to an immediate situation, like at a party. However, having joy in my life is more of a long-term decision I have made.

"The thief comes only to steal and kill and destroy. I came that they may have life and have it abundantly" (John 10:10).

This lie deals with voices from the past and is a boundary issue of how I measure myself with others. God does not want individuals to hide behind anything except Him. Through therapy, I learned God values me as His beloved son. I am important to Him.

I found people who value me, and I stay in contact with them. I meet with certain men who hold me accountable for my actions and attitude; I have male role models who have integrity and walk with God.

DR. SYDNEY: The lie: "Deep down in the core of my being, I have this intense self-hatred that demands punishment and/or sabotage."

JERRY: God created me as a sensitive, caring person with deep feelings. I believe God has redeemed the evil deeds and wrong choices that stole my identity. I no longer fear expressing my feelings. God made me feel alive with passion and expression.

My family made me stuff my feelings and believe something was wrong with me for having what God gave me. It must have broken His heart to see me believe this lie and focus my energy into destroying myself by thinking I was worthless and evil. God said to me, "Jerry, do not disdain yourself." God sees me as His beloved son in whom He is well pleased. He wants me to expect good and not evil.

I dishonor God when I disassociate to escape. God wants me to be a safe person. He has forgiven me for my perversions and is transforming my mind, releasing me from illegitimate use of that which He gave me. I am free to be myself, and I know that God loves me regardless of how I feel. With a healthy fear of God and using appropriate boundaries, I choose to be spontaneous, passionate, vulnerable, and happy in experiencing the abundant life promised me.

My Wycliffe family believed in God's work in me and in my family when I did not. Through counseling, I took a long, hard look at my life from the beginning. I did not like what I saw, but it produced two options: either suicide or yielding to God when I did not trust Him.

I believed everything I did was a failure. I didn't know who I was, and I had no dreams of the good life. Everything about me, God severely shook, breaking everything, exposing the foundation. That foundation was Christ, and at times I doubted my salvation. I knew deep down in my heart God loved me, yet during this time of chaos, I even had trouble remembering that.

The journey of finding who I am seems never to stop. I see God working in the background, unseen but present, and graciously extending mercy and grace to me in my search for finding myself.

Dr. Sydney: Jerry, good job. Our time is up for today. We will continue next week. See you then.

Your homework is to find answers to, "Is it safe and okay for me to be a separate person?" and "Can I exist on my own?"

Session 11—Continued Our Beliefs

Dr. Sydney: Jerry, welcome back. Let's start this session with a few more lies and your responses.

The lie: "When I feel overwhelmed, I shut down emotionally and disassociate myself from danger."

Jerry: In the past, there weren't safe people or places for me to be when those around me abused, rejected, or shamed me, or when life was overwhelming. There is safety in the arms of Jesus from all my abuse and everything that overwhelms me. I can escape to Jesus and not have to shut down emotionally or pretend I am someone else. I am free to be myself, and I know that Jesus loves me regardless of how I feel. When I am afraid, I will trust in the Lord.

DR. SYDNEY: The lie: "My lot in life is to stay a slave to ancestral curses and family patterns."

JERRY: I am claiming my birthright and not surrendering to anyone other than Jesus. I am trading abandonment, deception, rejection, finances, performance, mental problems, and anxiety for goodness and mercy. Jesus and I are closing the door and cleaning my house of ancestral curses and unhealthy family patterns. Jesus has set me free from the power of sin and death. My family and I are no longer slaves to the past, and I can live day to day without fear of evil because Jesus is right here with me, guarding and guiding me all the way.

"Even though I walk through the valley of the shadow of death, I will fear no evil, for You are with me; Your rod and Your staff, they comfort me" (Psalm 23:4).

Is it safe and okay for me to be a separate person? I have no clear definition of me, and I repeatedly ask myself who I am. Can I exist on my own? Alternatively, do I identify with you? I need to be a unique person, completely capable of standing on my own. Is it safe for me to be okay? Do I tend to sabotage myself since I do not feel safe and okay?

Co-dependency is enmeshment with someone else. Do I know who I am or whoever you say I am? Negative thoughts are deceptive and unhealthy. These include feelings of rejection, abandonment, emotional or physical pain, engulfment, and fear of the unknown. Positive thoughts are acceptance, security, healing, and a safe place. Positive thoughts are healthy. There are goals that positive thoughts have. One is a healthy perception of self as an entity; another is a robust definition of limitations and is a healthy sense of identification and safety. God does not say, "I will let you off the hook because you did not know my laws."

In his book Hiding from Love, author John Townsend illustrated this with a parable of a young girl who witnessed the murder of her family by rebel government forces, and she was the only one who escaped. After the war, this girl was afraid to come out of hiding. She saw military people looking for her and falsely believed they were the enemy, even though they were friends of the family coming to take her to safety. "I thought this about God: I witnessed the civil war in my life and the terrible things done to me by the enemy. Everyone was the enemy, not knowing God was the one calling me to come out of hiding and find safety and love."

Do not mock God. Feeble attempts to protect ourselves from harm exhibit a lack of faith in Him. Masks we wear to protect us misplace trust. As a little child, I had no protection from my parents and other family members. I did not know feelings had hooks. They consist of habits, compulsion, obsessive compulsion, and addiction. I am beginning to understand why it was so difficult for me to break out of a bad habit. I still had a hook attached to my lustful thought-life that kept me bound to those thoughts.

DR. SYDNEY: Jerry, I am amazed at you. You made those true and false statements look easy. I know how much hard work that takes for my clients to accomplish. Thank you so much.

There are ten ways parents damage a child's self-esteem.[50] We will look at these to get a better understanding of how the inner child was damaged.

1. Comparing kids with siblings or other children:

Comparing your kids to others is the ill-fated strategy of child-rearing. Instead, parents should focus on their kids' strong points and minimize the negative aspects. Kids are growing up and need positive attention, care, and understanding. Make sure they get it.

2. Criticizing your kid's behaviors, natural abilities, and temperament:

Parents should focus more on their kid's needs. Even if your child is different, it doesn't mean they are on the wrong track and need immediate correction. A successful strategy is to encourage kids to reveal their all-around personality and express their views.

3. Hinder individuality:

The most important thing is to encourage kids to think outside the box and develop their potential to the fullest. The task of every parent is to help kids develop their creative potential and unique talents.

4. Regularly harp about mistakes:

Parents need to teach their offspring not to be afraid of failures and future challenges. It is important to encourage kids to have a positive attitude toward their mistakes and explain that it is only the process of learning and gaining experience.

5. Assure that kids' goals, dreams, and desires are impossible to reach:

Teach them never to give up and always accomplish their goals. Parents should make it clear that nothing is impossible and if a kid wants to achieve something, the sky is the limit for their ambitions. The task of every parent is to help kids develop a winning attitude and approach to goal setting.

6. Make decisions for kids:

Parents need to steer their kids in the right direction, helping them make choices and decisions in their day-to-day lives. It is essential for kids to know the right way of decision-making. Once they know how to jump to the correct conclusion and make a right decision, it facilitates their confidence and encourages healthy risk-taking.

7. Evaluating kids' intellectual abilities based on their GPA: Never do that.

Parents shouldn't dwell on their kids' grades, making it the determining factor for their happiness. Instead, help your kids develop writing and listening skills, which are crucial when it comes to their studies. Give them your assistance in their studying and avoid pressure to get good grades.

8. Putting much weight on negative points:

Instead of pointing out kids' drawbacks, parents need to help them find their strong points and develop positive characteristics. It is essential to teach kids that nobody is perfect and making mistakes is a natural part of the learning process.

9. Never praising:

First, parents need to create a positive environment where kids feel they are loved and valued. Second, reinforce positive behavior and praise your kids when they do something well. It doesn't mean that parents need to praise kids for every little thing they do. As a parent, you need to develop a pattern of praise based on your child's achievements. It will help to establish competence and a positive attitude toward their own actions.

10. Demand blind obedience:

Instead, kids need to be listened to, and their points of view should be taken into consideration. Give your kid space for creativity and self-expression. Also, encourage kids to develop their own individuality, respecting parental opinions.

There are many ways parents can help kids improve their self-image and self-esteem.[51] Here are some of them:

1. Give them freedom of choice.

2. Don't do everything for them.

3. Give age-appropriate chores.

4. Let your child make mistakes.

5. Give them your love and care.

For every parent, it is crucial to raise kids with healthy self-esteem, and the work starts from the first days of their lives. Every child is different, and their future directly depends on the way they are brought up. Following the tips above, parents will be able to build their kids' self-esteem, raising happy and successful individuals.

CHAPTER 5

SESSIONS 12–14

The Inner Child

SESSION 12—THE IMPORTANCE OF THE FIRST FIVE YEARS OF LIFE

Childhood Development[52]

Children grow and develop at different rates, but most will reach several milestones between three and five. Developmental milestones can help identify when a child is struggling and provide direction to find out why. Children who are not meeting milestones and are struggling to learn may need additional supports to help them prepare for kindergarten. And with preschools currently closed because of the ongoing global pandemic, hundreds of thousands of children do not have access to the vital resources they need to hit their developmental milestones.

There are areas of development that are essential skills for children to have to build a strong foundation for learning.

When dealing with the inner child, the child will respond positively to reparenting using good thoughts and lots of love. To discipline a child, discuss with him when and where he can act out. He needs to know the boundaries and the consequences for being disobedient and the rewards for being obedient. If the child shows you little respect, think of ways to honor the child. Show the child love, kindness, and respect regardless of how he responds to you. He will pick up on your tone of voice. Remember, body language speaks louder than words. A role model to the child is a healthy way of responding to something terrible or something useful.

You teach the child positive manners.

117

1. Maintain a healthy, positive attitude toward the inner child. Reframe negative emotions toward the child.

2. Mere acceptance: Coexistence translates what the child especially needs.

3. Attention equals love, or even rejection equals love, where the child seeks out those who will reject him or her.

I want to share with you the difference between punishment and chastening. The purpose is different for each.

Discipline equals correction.

Correction equals growth.

Growth equals rehabilitation.

Rehabilitation equals punishment.

Four Simple Ways to Work with Your Inner Child

1. Speak to your inner child. Acknowledge your inner child and let it know you are there for it.

2. Look at pictures of yourself as a child.

3. Re-create what you loved to do as a child.

4. Make an inner journey—one of the most powerful ways to reconnect with your inner child.

Six Steps to Help Heal Your Inner Child

1. Trust

2. Validation

3. Shock & Anger

4. Sadness

5. Remorse

6. Loneliness

Say These Seven Things to Heal and Nurture Your Inner Child:

1. I love you.

2. I am listening to you.

3. You did not deserve this.

4. I am sorry.

5. I forgive you.

6. Thank you.

7. You did your best.

How do you respect the inner child? Love: give to get to give to get, etc. You can be the wife of a happy husband. You can be the husband of a happy wife.

It is not so important the time you spend with the child as that you do it. Must register that it is done.

The inner child does not know when the alarm is true or false, and it is just as alarming as genuine danger and threat. The inner child needs to be updated that the threat no longer exists in some way. So, communication between the adult and child. Just because we get false alarms, do not yank out the warning. God gave us a fire marshal inside us (our minds), so we can set limits, like no corporal punishment or temper tantrums, etc. Solve most problems by making a game out of it and play the kid out.

Jerry, when you want to write to Little Jerry Wayne, you will use your dominant hand; when the child communicates with you, you'll use your non-dominant hand; the writing resembles a child's writing.

"Dear Little Jerry Wayne, I never want to hurt you again. I want you to be part of me. I am sorry for all I did to you. Will you forgive me?"

The Importance of Forgiveness

"Forgive." That word can strike terror in many people's hearts. How do I? How can I, after all that has happened?

Perhaps you have suffered unspeakable harm; perhaps you are the one who inflicted the pain. The events may even seem to justify a lasting resentment against another or yourself. Justice may cry out from the pain, but mercy cries out to God. And God requires forgiveness.

Forgiveness is the bedrock on the pathway to healing. Biblical forgiveness flows in three essential directions: forgiving others, receiving forgiveness from our heavenly Father, and forgiving ourselves. If unforgiveness is present, God's hand of protection, mercy, and restoration is hindered, at best, and, at worst, halted.

While we must decide to forgive, forgiveness is more than a decision; it must come from the heart. That takes God's grace; it takes God's healing. We cannot always start by forgiving from our heart, but we can begin by deciding to forgive. Then, as we enter onto a healing pathway, our decision to forgive will be more and more from our heart, and the wounds of our heart will be more and more healed. If we persevere, God can and will bring us to the place of wholehearted forgiveness.

WE ARE ENTERING THE WORLD OF LITTLE JERRY WAYNE

SESSION 13—THE INNER CHILD

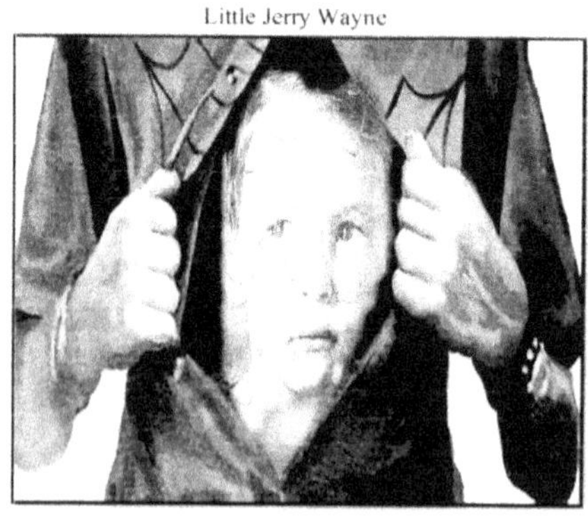

My inner child, Little Jerry Wayne

Housecat is looking in the mirror and sees a lion looking back.

Jerry Wayne drew this picture, age 6

JERRY: With my friend Anton Fleischman's help, I identified the cruel events inflicted upon me as a small child. These experiences are not socially acceptable, and therefore needed to be hidden as the Jerry Wayne years. Although I disowned Jerry Wayne, he lurked in the shadows, causing me extreme discomfort as I tried to live the good Christian life, a life that did not allow Jerry Wayne to exist, or so I thought.

I realized that Jerry Wayne does exist, and only by bringing him into the light of the conscious mind could I deal with that part of me. But I did not visit Jerry Wayne alone; Jesus was with me. With the help of Scriptures, I saw the real Jerry Wayne. By understanding and appreciating him, I am becoming a complete person, that beautiful person God planned for me before I was created. Instead of being a disreputable beast, the Dark Pony has been transformed into a white thoroughbred stallion capable of carrying me into the spiritual battles Jesus has equipped me to fight.

Little Jerry Wayne drew a lovely picture of Dark Pony when he was six years old.

DARK PONY

Poem by Jerry Wayne

Dark Pony, who are you? When you look in the mirror, what do you see? What matters most is how you see yourself. A brilliant stallion tested and right; it is he, the one looking back at you. Brilliant stallion, what do you see when you are looking back at me? I see you, and I like what I see. When I look into your eyes, I see the fear of fear that made you cringe. When I look into your eyes, I see teardrops of sorrows. Dark Pony's transformation to Brilliant Stallion was painful. Change is death to the old and life to the new; the struggle so intense, but you did it and emerged as the beautiful creature you are today.

I see the obstacles of the dark side of life as steppingstones to a bright future. The trials and pitfalls do not scare you as before. You embrace life differently as you journey close to God; with all your heart, you look the storm straight in its face. The things that caused you to fall now help you walk without stumbling over life. You lean on God. He is your compass, your concrete foundation, your safe place, and your companion. Your perception changed. You no longer ask the questions, "How do I see myself?" "How do I see the world around me?" "How do others see me?"

Perception is your point of view about yourself, how you think others see you. You will run just as fast if you believe a bear is after you as you would if it were true, and one was after you. To change your perception results in death to the old way of thinking and life to your new perspective. Like the magical bird in ancient stories, the phoenix rises from the ashes of the past. There can be no growth without change and no change without letting go of the former. Transforming a dark pony into a brilliant stallion has involved pain and death to old dreams.

Suppose I am with a friend, and we see the bear. If my attitude was, I don't have to outrun the bear, just my friend, I sure hope my friend doesn't think that way too!

Do I base my actions on my needs and goals, or is my behavior depending on how I believe others see me? My perception is how I see myself and how I perceive my surrounding world. Another perception is how others view my world and me. I have no control over others' view of me, but I can control how I perceive my world and myself. If you want to keep up with me, you had better fasten your seatbelt now as we ride this emotional roller coaster. We are entering the world of Jerry Wayne, facing the storms of life head-on with God by my side.

As I journey from life to death, I pass through the wilderness valley with its narrow paths and craggy rocks. I must embrace these problematic places. Either I take sorrow and suffering as my guides or I circumvent the deep work God does for me as I know Him intimately, walking by faith and not by sight. I deliberately choose the narrow way. I do not care what the crowd does. They choose the way of peace and ease. On my journey, Jesus is first in my life. With Jesus first, I can love others and bring them with me to Him.

As I sojourn with God, I have healing and redemption, more perspective, purpose, and passion in life. As I sojourn with God, I have the redemption of my doubt and betrayal, disappointment, and ambivalence. As I sojourn with God, He calls me to become a man of faith, hope, and love.

Can I daily experience the presence of Almighty God? Scripture is clear I can approach His majestic presence only by the blood of Jesus, acknowledging my sinfulness and accepting Jesus as my Lord and Savior. When I do that, I can walk once again in the cool of the day with God because of the sacrificial work of Jesus on the cross. I am encouraged to draw near to God, where I can significantly admire His glorious presence. The Shekinah glory of God is over the Mercy Seat. God is inviting me into His presence. This is an incredible privilege, invited to enter the very presence of Almighty God because of Christ's work!

Since we have the confidence to enter the holy places by the blood of Jesus, by the new and living way that He opened for us through the curtain, and since we have a great priest over the house of God, let us draw near with a real heart in full assurance of faith, with our hearts sprinkled clean from an evil conscience and our bodies washed with pure water.

"And He has said to me, 'My grace is sufficient for you, for power is perfected in weakness.' Most gladly, therefore, I will rather boast about my weaknesses so that the power of Christ may dwell in me" (2 Corinthians 12:9–10).

DR. SYDNEY: The part in your poem about the bear reminds me of a funny story I want to tell you.

The Christian Bear

An atheist was hiking through the woods one day, admiring the beauty of nature. What majestic trees; what mighty rivers! What beautiful animals! he said to himself. As he walked alongside the river, he heard a rustling in the bushes behind him. He turned to look and saw a seven-foot grizzly charging toward him. The man ran as fast as he could up the path. He looked over his shoulder and saw the bear was even closer. Then the man tripped and fell to the ground. He rolled over to pick himself up but saw that the bear was right on top of him, reaching for him with his left paw and raising his right paw to strike him.

At that instant, the atheist cried out, "Oh, my God!"

Time stopped; the bear froze; the forest was silent. As a bright light shone upon the man, a thundering voice came out of the sky, "You deny my existence for all these years, teach others I don't exist, and even credit creation to a cosmic accident. Do you expect me to help you out of this predicament? Am I to count you as a believer?"

The atheist looked directly into the light and said, "It would be hypocritical of me to ask you to treat me as a Christian now, suddenly, but perhaps you could make the bear a Christian?"

"Very well," said the voice.

The light went out, the sounds of the forest resumed, and the bear dropped his right paw, brought both paws together, bowed his head, and spoke, "Lord, bless this food which I am about to receive from thy bounty. Through Christ our Lord, amen."

The type of attachment between a parent and a child profoundly impacts how a child's brain is developed. If a parent can provide a secure attachment, they have a relationship with their child where the child feels connected, secure, and protected. The child is sure and knows they can count on their parent to consistently meet their needs. Not all the time, not entirely, but for the most part they know the parent will be there. When the child has this experience repeatedly, it allows the brain to wire the expectation for other relationships. It also develops the frontal lobe, the part of the brain that allows us to have empathy, be flexible, understand ourselves, communicate well with others, have all kinds of excellent and powerful ways to make decisions, and be successful. Whereas Little Jerry Wayne had parents who were only inconsistently available to him, who brushed him off, and dismissed his emotional state. In that case, his brain got wired to expect that others wouldn't be there consistently to meet his needs.

Jerry: I wrote this poem, called These are My Memory Pains:

Let me be somebody; let me be me. Why can I not be me?
You are not smart enough.

I hate myself and desire to be someone else. No one says to me "I love you." What is wrong with me?

I do not want to live and wish I were dead. I am so lonely.

I do not feel safe; some of these people scare me. They say bad things about me. I do not trust them. Some have hurt me, and I do not like them. They say bad things to me and make me cry.

I promise myself I will not be like that when I get big.

You ignore me, except when you whip me. You treat me as if I had no mind and no feelings. Would you miss me if I were gone?

I have no dream of the future, but one thing I know, I do not want to grow up to be like you.

I ache with pain as if this were only yesterday. I pretend all is well.

I am all grown up now. Why do I feel like a little boy needing to hide? I was not safe then, and I am not safe now.

Dr. Sydney: Your poem describes to me what it was like when you were little. Jerry, my mother used to say, "A penny for your thoughts." Will you describe your thoughts, what are you thinking right now?

Jerry: Right now, I feel sad for the way I treated Little Jerry Wayne. I went back to Jerry Wayne's world and returned with Little Jerry Wayne. Now that Little Jerry Wayne was out of the closet (the cellar), I became best friends with him. We did fun things together and talked about what we wanted to do and the dreams we dared to have. All this was new to Little Jerry Wayne.

Time passed quickly, and Little Jerry Wayne is a teenager. This was another horrible time for him, as he was never prepared to face life in the city with more abuse and shame. In a sense, this stage of life was more challenging and hurt more than being a child.

Now he has grown up with good feelings about himself. The challenging work I did over the past few weeks paid off. We enjoy each other.

What happens when we do not feel as safe as children? I coped with life by pretending I was someone else, my alter ego, Dark Pony! When I was little, I used to pretend I was someone else when the abuse was occurring. I saw myself as a little pony that would gallop away to a safe distance and watch the exploitation. I deadened my feelings. I called myself Dark Pony, and I daydreamed about being someone else every time I was abused. Mother caught my sister and me in the act and accused me of starting it. I was passive. It was not me, even though we both got a whipping with the razor strap. Thus, Dark Pony represented the cruel events inflicted upon me as a small child. I identified this period of life as the "Little Jerry Wayne years."

I like this picture of a golden-colored house cat looking in a mirror, and the face reflected back to him is a majestic lion. The caption is: "What matters most is how you see yourself." It goes with my poem, Dark Pony. Thus, the phrase in my poem, "I see you, and I like what I see."

DR. SYDNEY: Safety is not just physical, but emotional, psychological, and spiritual. When we feel genuinely safe within our family environment, we have our physical and emotional boundaries respected. Our authentic selves are accepted. We feel close to and loved by our family members (most notably our parents). We also need to be permitted to grow and change and have all our basic physical necessities met (food, water, a safe home, or neighborhood).

LITTLE JERRY WAYNE (LJW): Are you there, Jerry? I am lonely. Will you play with me? Can we draw a picture and color it?

JERRY: Yes, we can draw a picture and color it. What would you like to draw?

LJW: Will you help me draw a picture of a happy me?

(They draw a picture.)

Jerry drew the picture of Little Jerry Wayne, age 7, and Little Jerry Wayne painted it.

JERRY: Little Jerry, I am so proud of you. You did such a lovely job. Would you like to do this again some other time?

LJW: Yes. I knew it would be hard, but I did it. Jerry let's do it again.

JERRY: Okay, I will draw and you color.

DR. SYDNEY: A person with a childlike attitude believes in God and accepts God as He is and has a willingness to obey God, but preconceived ideas make it difficult to believe in God. The religious leaders of Jesus's day did not have willing hearts to believe or a willingness to obey the Scriptures.

As we look back to the cross and Jesus's death over 2,000 years ago, we read Isaiah, and it is as if Isaiah was an eyewitness to Jesus's crucifixion and wrote the article for The Jerusalem Post the next day.

A WILLING HEART, BASED ON ISAIAH 52–53

Why did the religious leaders of Jesus's day miss who Jesus was? The Pharisees missed the essential prophecy fulfillment because they lacked a willingness to believe and act on God's Word.[53] To them, the Scriptures were a book to be studied, not a prescription for life. The critical prophecy the Pharisees missed is in Isaiah 61, listing Jesus's resume. Check for yourself His job description, and then compare that to any of these books: Matthew or Luke or Mark or John.

The things Jesus did were not one-time events. He did not make a big show of these things, but everyone in the Jewish world heard of them, especially the religious leaders. I believe what tripped them up were the additions added to the existing laws God gave, such as how far a person could walk or what qualified as work on the Sabbath. They witnessed the miracles and knew they were supernatural occurrences, but their minds were so full of their misinterpretation of Scripture, there was no room for the Holy Spirit to work within them.

A familiar story that illustrates this principle is told about a high-minded man who visits a monk, seeking to achieve enlightenment.[54] The monk hands the man a cup and begins to pour tea into it. As the cup fills, the tea splashes out, soaking the man's feet and the floor. The startled man asks the monk what he thinks he is doing. The monk replies that this cup is just like the man's mind. Because it is already filled with his ideas, there is no room for anything more unless he empties it first.

This is a story about the need for surrender and illustrates Christ's teaching on Christians needing to come as children, be childlike, to receive. The inference here is that children are open to learning, whereas we have already filled our minds with what we want to believe.

"The Spirit of the Lord God is upon me, because the Lord anointed me to bring good news to the humble. He has sent me to bind up the brokenhearted, to proclaim release to captives and freedom to prisoners; to proclaim the favorable year of the Lord and the day of vengeance of our God. To comfort all who mourn, to grant those who mourn in Zion, giving them a garland instead of ashes, the oil of gladness instead of mourning, the cloak of praise instead of a disheartened spirit. So, they will be called oaks of righteousness, the planting of the Lord that He may be glorified." The prophet Isaiah gave this job description of the Messiah one-thousand years before His birth.

Is it possible to study the Bible without getting to know God? Yes! Think about this: The religious leaders of Jesus's day fiercely opposed Him, yet they were ardent students of the Bible. They had long portions of Scripture memorized. They could debate every possible meaning, yet they did not recognize Jesus as the Messiah, the anointed one. Why?

Jesus explained it this way to them: "You search the Scriptures because you think that you have eternal life; it is these that testify about Me; and you are unwilling to come to Me so that you may have life. I do not receive glory from men; but I know you, that you do not have a love of God in yourselves. I have come in My Father's name, and you do not receive Me; if another comes in his name, you will receive him. How can you believe when you receive glory from one another, and you do not seek the glory that is from the one and only God? Do not think that I will accuse you before the Father; the one who accuses you is Moses, in whom you have set your hope. For if you believed Moses, you would believe Me, for he wrote about Me. But if you do not believe his writings, how will you believe My words?" (John 5:39–47).

We must approach the Bible with faith, as God's living voice to us. But it does not stop there. We must have a willingness to act on the things God shows us. If we are unwilling to modify our daily lives to line up with God's truths, we will quickly lose our desire to listen to God's voice.

"If anyone is willing to do His will, he will know of the teaching, whether God or I speak from Myself" (John 7:17).

Jesus is speaking of our willingness and decision to do what God wants, regardless of our feelings about His truths. If you want to enjoy Bible study and hear God's voice speaking to you personally through the Bible, then you must be willing to act on the things He shows you; this is essential heart preparation for meaningful Bible study. Take courage, friend. If you know you lack willingness, you are where God can help you the most. Tell Him all your reservations, surrender them to Him, and trust that He will change you. Begin by praying, "Lord, I am willing to be made willing." Then watch out because He will do it!

He will transform you by renewing your mind, that you may prove what the good and acceptable and perfect will of God is—Romans 12:2.

Accurate knowledge of the Bible can be gained only through the aid of the Spirit by whom the Word was given. To gain this knowledge, we must live by it. All that God's Word commands, we are to obey, and all that it promises, we may claim. Only as the Bible is thus held can it be studied effectively.

Jerry, your homework is to make an acrostic of Little Jerry Wayne.

SESSION 14—REPARENTING THE INNER CHILD

DR. SYDNEY: Heavenly Father, please make this time we have together a blessing as Jerry learns who he is and how to become healthy. Refresh him and still any storms that come to prevent Jerry from progressing into the man you see in him. Help him not be discouraged. In Jesus's name, amen.

We are using 1 Corinthians 13:11 on which to base our inner-child work. It says that when a person becomes a man, he no longer thinks and acts like he did when a child. Now he matures and thinks and acts like a man. Since you are no longer a child, we need to help those childhood memories heal and become healthy.

Your inner child needs to know that it's okay to "be."

Jerry, please share your acrostic with the name you gave your inner child.

ACROSTIC—LITTLE JERRY WAYNE ROBINSON

L = Learning To Trust God More

I = In God I Trust

T = Trading My Sorrows For Joy

T = Taking Time For God; Turning Lose Of The Control Of My Life
     To Jesus

L = Loving Others Is Sometimes Hard To Do

E = Engaging With Others On A More Personal Level

J = Justified And Redeemed/ Joint Heir With Christ

E = Earnestly Following God

R = Ready And Available For Whatever Comes

R = Realizing God Is With Me

Y = Yesterday Is Behind Me, Tomorrow Is Before Me

W = Wonderful Being Full Of Awe And Appreciation

A = Actively Engaging In Bible Study

Y = Yearning To Do God's Will

N = Never Give Up On Jesus

E = Everlasting Life Is Mine

R = Respect Little Jerry Wayne As An Important Part Of My Life

O = Owning Little Jerry Wayne

B = Building New Memories With Little Jerry Wayne

I = Involving Little Jerry Wayne In All Areas Of My Life

N = Nurturing Little Jerry Wayne

S = Sharing Lots Of Love With Little Jerry Wayne

O = Overcome Fear

N = Never Give Up On Little Jerry Wayne

Childishness vs. Childlikeness
Matthew 18:2–5, Characteristics of
Matthew 19:13–14, Characteristics of

Childlikeness	Childishness:
Trusting	Winning
Gentle	Bully
Respectful	Selfish
Laughing	Crying

1. Which of these things did you never or seldom do as a child?

2. Which of these things did you do a lot? Which did you enjoy a lot?

3. Which of these things (or other things children do) would you probably enjoy doing as an adult?

4. How do you feel when you think about doing something childlike as an adult?

Meaningful early childhood experiences determine whether you grow up to be a healthy person or an emotional mess. You must know how to cope in an adult world where you are faced with choices every day. In childhood, you practice the skills you will need as an adult. It all goes back to how you were raised, because you will model the way you were raised, whether in a healthy home or an unhealthy one. You need to learn social skills before you are a grown-up. How one grows up relates to the world, and how one is free to make choices to shape one's own life is learned from the parents.

"At that time, the disciples came to Jesus and said, 'Who then is greatest in the kingdom of heaven?' And He called a child to Himself and set him before them and said, 'Truly I say to you, unless you are converted and become like children, you will not enter the kingdom of heaven. Whoever then humbles himself as this child, he is the greatest in the kingdom of heaven. And whoever receives one such child in My name receives Me; but whoever causes one of these little ones who believe in Me to stumble, it would be better for him to have a heavy millstone hung around his neck and to be drowned in the depth of the sea'" (Matthew 18:1–6).

Then some children were brought to Him so that He might lay His hands on them and pray, and the disciples rebuked them. But Jesus said, 'Let the children alone, and do not hinder them from coming to Me; for the kingdom of heaven belongs to such as these.' After laying His hands on them, He departed from there" (Matthew 19:13–15).

Has God ever asked you to do something during your Bible study time? What did you do? How did He bless you?

Jerry, your homework is to make a collage of the positive things you want in your life.

Hello, Jerry. Let us pray. Heavenly Father, thank you for blessing our time together and for the good work you are doing in Jerry's life. Amen.

Jerry, please share your collage.

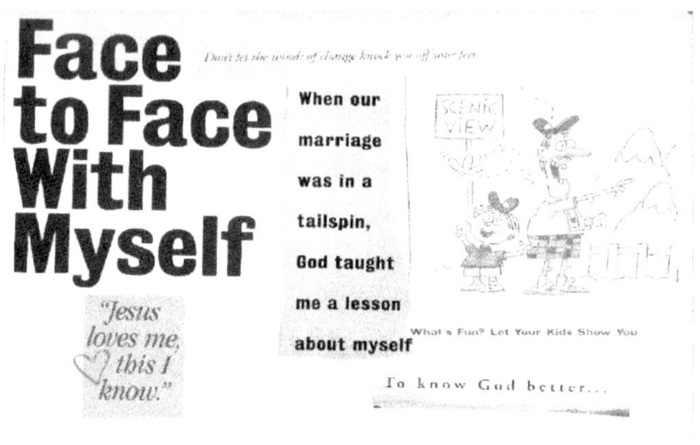

CHAPTER 6

SESSIONS 15–17

Barriers

Session 15—Barriers Affecting Living

Dr. Sydney: As individuals, we erect emotional walls around us. We use self-made bricks. We have walls that are so deep in our conscious minds, we are unaware they are there until somebody violates our invisible space. Then we explode with such a fierce reaction it surprises us. We are like water in a pot that simmers on the heat and is ready to erupt into a vigorous boil. Until that point, we didn't know we had a boundary wall of protection. The invisible boundaries were put in place by us when we were little and trying to make sense of the world. Our parents assisted us in forming our bricks, or we did the best we could without help.

Suppose that person had healthy relationships with parents and significant others. He could build a healthy personality and set goals. He knew how to handle himself in public and interact with others in appropriate ways. He knew how to choose between good and evil. He faced new challenges with confidence.

On the other hand, the person emotionally wounded in early childhood did whatever he could to keep himself safe. Splitting his personality into a safe mode despite the abuse occurring to him, he could escape by becoming someone else in his mind. He could watch the damage and have no feelings. Alternatively, he might turn to drugs or alcohol to medicate himself. By the time this person is an adolescent, he is troubled, rebellious, defiant to authority, and unable to interact socially. He is dependent on others and has issues with mental health.

"Do not move the ancient boundary or go into the fields of the fatherless, for their Redeemer is strong; He will plead their case against you" (Proverbs 23:10–11).

First, we will compare the emotional boundaries to physical boundaries because the physical is more comfortable to visualize. There are barriers to communication, social norms, cross-cultural relationships, and perception.

If we have a pet dog, we build a fence to keep it safe on our property. We have geographical boundaries for our land. We have title deeds that prove this is our property. We have airspace for recreational hobbies and commercial airliners.

Some of us do not know about our personal space. We know we feel uncomfortable when someone gets close to us, not realizing we have a barrier. Physical walls include bumper guards on the sides of our highways, property rights, and civil laws. Without a survey of property boundaries, no one can be sure that this piece of land is his or not. To keep others from stealing part of their land or using the land unacceptably, homeowners' associations establish rules for the people living in that area to guide them whenever they need to expand or make changes to their real estate or home. The same is true with villages, towns, and cities. We have the governing body we elect to represent us in these places; this applies to county, state, and national government. The enforcement of the law either prosecutes or defends us in the court.

Then people like-minded in thoughts and actions become a group that has boundaries or rules to keep them together. They hold people obedient to their goals and kick out those who disobey. Genesis 6 was a perfect example of when like-minded people got together, resulting in murder, rape, and stealing. Lust and greed controlled their perverted thinking.

Humankind uses walls to keep something inside or keep something outside. In our individual lives, we do the same thing. You don't want me to know your secret deeds and thoughts, and I don't want everybody knowing my secret acts and beliefs. We hide behind our built walls.

JERRY: I have been searching for meaning in my life, finding my place and purpose for why I am here. What do I want in life? How did I get so messed up?

Dr. Sydney: You've got to know with clarity what you want and be prepared to tune and tweak as you go. You must learn and earn if you want to turn and burn! You can learn from my mistakes and my success to create a life you love full of fast times, fun, and freedom. Listen to your heart and let it carry you in the direction of your dreams. To get what you want, you have to know what you want, and why, with great clarity, and you have to commit to it. As you work on your plan, it is essential to be open and willing to receiving divine guidance and redirect your course as necessary. At the same time, do not get distracted by what you want right now and lose sight of what you want most.

A goal without a plan is just a wish. —Antoine de Saint-Exupery

The meaning of the idiom, learn, earn, burn:

Learn = to know what you want, your purpose; to discover or become informed about someone or something, after one has learned something from personal experience.

Earn = to prove one's skill in a particular area.

Burn = you have more that is required or expected.

Without a purpose, it is easy to pursue things that you think you should be doing.

Existence is a strange bargain. Life owes us little; we owe it everything. —William Cowper

According to Deepak Chopra, M.D., founder of The Chopra Foundation and co-founder of The Chopra Center for Wellbeing, what most people find when they look inside themselves are:

1. Confusion: manifests as not setting clear priorities because the path ahead doesn't look clear and decisive.

2. Distraction: manifests as a hundred small things that pull your attention this way and that.

3. Disorganization: manifests as a lack of orderly thinking that leads to productive results.

4. Transparency: Most people's lives are still not transparent. It is a struggle almost every adult goes through. What do I want to do with my life? What do I not suck at? Millions of people have no clue what they want to do with themselves, and that is okay.

No assessment is going to provide you with immediate clarity and a sense of purpose. Seeking clarity in uncertain times can be a daunting experience, and it can be stressful if the solutions you seek don't appear when you need them.

5. Self-discovery is a journey!

There is no better feeling than suddenly becoming clear on something that had previously been a roadblock in your life. Those "aha!" moments are a real blessing when they come. The only journey is the one within, says Rainer Maria Rilke.

A. A strong sense of purpose fuels your motivation.

B. Clarity of purpose changes everything.

Your purpose in life is to find and do the things that bring glory and honor to God, making you smile, laugh, and forget time. Even if you are not sure yet, move into the exploration and experimentation phase of your life and enjoy the journey. You cannot put time into it. You cannot force yourself to find your why tomorrow or next month, or even next year. But search for clarity as you go with God. He will direct your way. (Proverbs 3:5–6.)

Each one of us has our own castle of mud or sand. Each one of us has our imaginary fortress and our own set of emotional baggage that took deep root inside our hearts. We all needed new management to transform the old patterns of living into steppingstones to the future, free from emotional baggage. The following are patterns affecting how we live.

When we refer to landmarks, we mean the four points of your personality that define who you are. We all know somebody who is a mess emotionally. These are good, genuine, sweet, caring people, but they are very troubled. They are examples of someone who had their boundaries violated as a child. One of the cruelest violations is sexual abuse. Many of these people have no memory of such behavior and actions done to them.

Do you know where to draw a line in relationships? Removing a pylon leaves a vacuum where the original markers were located. The enemy replaced the real pylons with false ones consisting of landmines instead of stones. When you perceive a threat, it serves as the trigger activating the explosive—whatever that is, whoever that is—which then triggers the emotional landmine.

Examine what you say and what you do; this will reveal what your belief system is. You seek self-worth, competence, belonging, or you seek to avoid rejection, abandonment, pain memory, experiencing pain over and over, engulfment, and fear of fear itself. When something good that should have happened did not happen, it produces an unmet need. When you are incapable of processing such occurrences in a positive spiritual, mental, emotional, and physical way, you produce unresolved issues that need processing. Those who come to Jesus for what He can do for them are hurt and disappointed; they do not come to Jesus because of who He is! They came to Jesus wanting a free handout.

A surveyor places stakes along your property line to separate it from the neighbors. Emotional landmarks have a similar purpose. I know where these stakes are. Am I me, or am I who you tell me I am? Your emotional property's four survey markers are:

1. Knowing who you are is one corner of your emotional self.

2. Knowing where other people are is another stake. Are they squatters on your property or did they steal some of your land?

3. The third corner of our emotional property is personal choice. You can make choices on your own, and others don't have the right to tell you what is best for you.

4. The fourth is you can use your property as you wish: build on it, plant a garden, or put livestock on it. It is your property to use as you choose. In Scripture, one example of boundaries is in Proverbs 24:30–34.

These are the survey markers that make you who you are. These stakes consist of either faith or fear.

Now, think with me how your parents raised you. This goes back to the four corner markers we just identified. You repeat after me:

Stake number one is knowing who you are.

Stake number two is knowing where other people are.

Stake three is knowing you have personal choices.

Stake four is how you intend to use your property; how you treat and care for yourself.

Besides defining you, these four stakes have one factor in common: how you were raised. Did you learn from your family to have good thoughts about who you are; did you feel secure? Did you learn and demonstrate relating to others appropriately?

Jerry, your homework is to compose an essay of barriers.

Session 16—How We Relate to Ourself and Others

Hi, Jerry. Let us pray. Dear Lord, Help Jerry understand the concept of Landmarks, Boundaries and Wall. Amen.

Jerry, please share your essay.

Jerry: I titled my essay "Building Clay Castles."

As a child, I built castles from clay after the thunderstorms passed over my Texas home. The sun baked; my villas were hard as brick. My significant others used hammers to smash my castles to bits. The routine: I built the fortifications, and they broke them down. I was powerless to protect my castles and suffered the loss of childhood innocence, trust, acceptance, and self-esteem. Soon I changed the building material.

Instead of using sand or clay, I built imaginary castles to keep myself safe. Physical abuse, sexual abuse, and emotional abuse broke my mental fortress, leaving me a psychological mess. I did not know who I was or where I fit in social situations. I learned to shut down emotionally by pretending I was someone else; my secret identity was Dark Pony.

As an adult, Dark Pony did not protect me. I used information given to me as a child by significant others to build my new stronghold. Not knowing I was using building blocks made of lies, I built it. My supplies were emotional bricks.

1. The watchtower of inherited dysfunction guarded the north side.

2. The watchtower of unrealistic expectations about my perception and station in life guarded the east side.

3. The watchtower of long-forgotten hurtful events, still raw, guarded the south side.

4. The watchtower of invisible spiritual entities oppressing me guarded the west side.

This fortress kept me safe, but I was a prisoner. I could not go out, and others couldn't come inside. Again, I was in a helpless situation and needed a workable refuge. I remembered God, humbled myself to Him, confessed my hopeless situation, and asked Him for help. He told me to take one brick from the wall and hand it to Him. He took the block, and I called it by name: the masonry of lack of faith, the brick of fear, the slab of anger, the masonry of jealousy, etc. I named each of the blocks used for constructing my stronghold, things in my life that developed into destructive roots, like crabgrass. These choked my life and my faith in God.

Then I focused my thoughts on God. I prayed for Him to rescue me, and instead of condemnation, He spoke love, hope, faith, and forgiveness to me. He spoke a new beginning.

"Bring my soul out of prison, so that I may give thanks to Your name; the righteous will surround me, for You will deal bountifully with me" (Psalm 142:7).

My children and I built sandcastles and watched the waves come to wash away part of them. We rebuilt and watched another wave come, again taking away parts. We spent hours at the beach and had a wonderful time playing together. My wife and I instilled excellent skills in our children. They did not fear the waves coming to wash away their play castles.

We wanted them to have coping skills when the giant waves came, so we taught them how to swim and enjoy the water without fear, how to respect the water and not swim in strong currents, how to watch for dangerous things in the water, and always to have someone with them. Some of our fondest memories as a family were our times together at the beach.

Dr. Sydney: As you read your essay, I could picture Little Jerry Wayne building his fortress. Well done. I will be teaching on the several types of barriers and what each does.

It is difficult to visualize something you can not see. When we talk about barriers, we are talking about the invisible boundaries. For example, when someone stands too close facing you, you feel uncomfortable. That uncomfortable feeling is telling you someone has violated your personal space. The two illustrations with circles represents you. Notice the rings inside the circles. You consist of five separate areas with it's own boundaries. Each of the five has it's own set of boundaries. Each of the four boundaries has it own set of pylons.

THERE ARE FIVE SETS OF BOUNDARIES: 1. SPIRITUAL; 2. PHYSICAL AND OR SEXUAL; 3. INTELLECTUAL; 4. SOCIAL AND PROFESSIONAL; 5. EMOTIONAL. YOU CAN BE IN ANY GIVEN RING, BUT ONLY IN ONE AT A TIME.

1. You are in the center ring. It's called the LOVE OR HATE circle. You either love or hate yourself.

2. The ring next to the center is called RESPECT. The only people in this ring are those who show you respect.

3. The third ring from the center is ACCEPTANCE. The only people in this ring are peers, classmates, coworkers, club members.

4. The fourth ring from the center is TOLERANCE.

5. The fifth ring is for STRANGERS.

5. The outside ring is your emotional boundary
4. The fourth ring is your social and professional boundaries
3. The third ring is your intellectual boundary
2. The second ring is your physical and sexual boundaries
1. The center ring is your spiritual boundary

These categories relate to our physical, emotional, social, spiritual, sexual, and intellectual life and can be illustrated by five circles, each within the other. The center circle is you, yourself, the next circle is your best friend, close relationships, your extended relationships, your coworkers or club associates, and the next circle relates to your occasional contacts.

HOW YOU RELATE:

Let us pretend you are a square: You have four corners These are the stakes at your four corners: You were born with four corners, and your parents defined these corners for you. If they did their God given responsible job of raising you in a healthy environment, you turned out to be a person of Faith. If they failed their God given responsible job of raising you in a healthy environment, your turned out to be a messed-up person of Fear. Faith or Fear defines you for the rest of your live. So, which are you, a person of Faith or a person of Fear?

1. knowing who you are

2. knowing where others are

3. knowing you have choices

4. knowing how you want to life your life

These four corners are formed during your first five years of life.

That is the reason we began your counseling sessions with defining your roots. These four corners are your roots. That is the reason your belief system is important for you to know. Your belief system is either based on Faith or Fear. Faith is the truths you tell yourself; fear is the false self-talk you tell yourself. I hope you are now seeing and understand that everything we have done in counseling relates to healthy inner child or the damaged inner child. This ties in with the landmarks, boundaries, and walls that identify how you relate to yourself, how you think about yourself, and how and why you relate to others. It is one whole package and defines who you are and how you got to be the way you are. That in a nutshell is the real you.

All this affects how you perceive yourself, your self-image and how you relate to one another.

We will now review.

Every part of us has its boundaries that specify where we start and finish. There are four corners to everything we are:

1. Knowing who we are

2. Knowing where others are

3. Knowing we have choices

4. Knowing how you want to use your space, land, work, play that these corner post identify

These four boundary markers were put in place when you were a child by your parents or primary care giver for the first five years of life. This is the reason those early years are vital to who you will become. Either you grew up with a satisfying healthy outlook where you have faith in yourself and handling new situations alright, or you grow up being fearful and unsure of yourself or abilities and are afraid of life. You can summarize who and what you do either a person of faith or a person of fear. The four corners apply to your emotional self, social (and sexual) self, you intellectual self, physical self, and spiritual self. I hope you are staying up with me so far. Now these five selves mentioned above, each has its individual set of it own four markers to identify where each starts and ends. These four sets of markers indicate how you relate to yourself, and to friends, and those that respect you, and strangers. The most important is You yourself-it is whether a love or hate relationship with yourself, You may include with yourself several other people who you trust wholeheartedly. The next group is friends that honor and respect you. Not included in the friends group are relatives that belittle you, put them in the next group. After the friends group comes associates and classmates who are acquainted with you and treat you with respect. The last group is those you hardly know, and strangers. Remember these four group each has its own set of boundary posts marking your property.

The core of who you are is based on FAITH or FEAR.

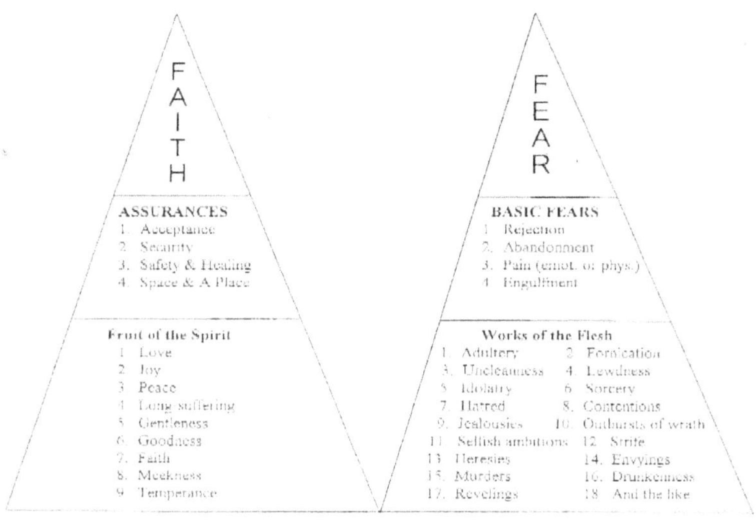

Examine the Word *FEAR*

Two purposes of infancy fears:
1. Survival (physical)

2. Felt need for parents

Two purposes for adult rational fears:
1. Survival (eternal)

2. Felt need for God -

Principles for overcoming irrational fears

Dr. Larry Gilham, L.P.C., L.M.F.T., C.S.C.
Little Flock Ministries (972) 594-1421

Remember this illustration; this is fundamental in how you think about yourself and why you do or do not relate well with others.

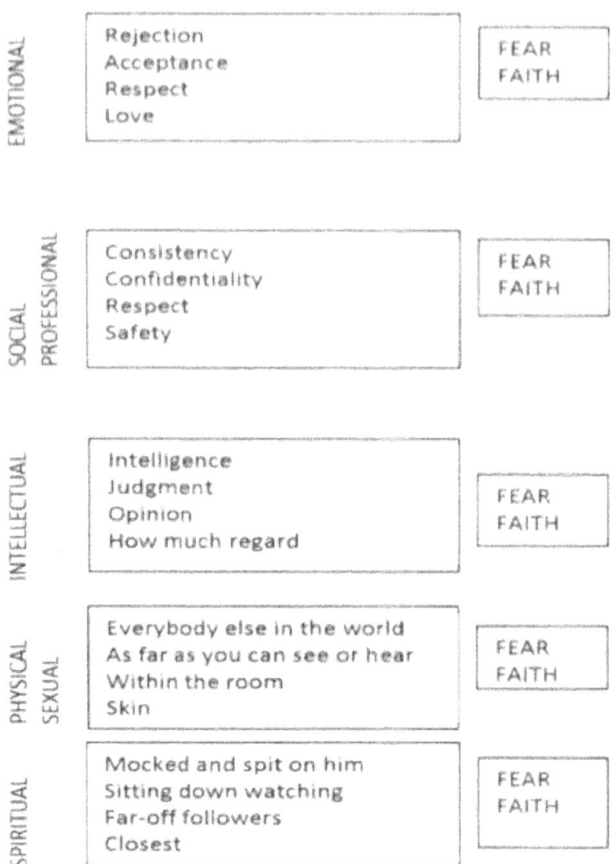

THE KEY POINTS:

1. the center is you. You relate to yourself in one of two ways. Either you love yourself, or you hate yourself. You may have as many as six other people in the center with you that you trust wholeheartedly.

2. next is how your relate to those you respect, close friends and loved ones. There can be as many as you respect and that show respect to you. If one of these does not respect you, remove that person to the outside of your respect circle.

3. those that you are friends with at school, club, church, sports, but not someone you can depend on. These are the ones you accept and who accept you.

4. the outside circle is for everybody else, strangers, people who you tolerate.

You have the right to move someone nearer you or farther away from you.

In Old Testament times, the property markers were called pylons, usually made of three layers of large stones stacked on time of each other forming a pyramid. The bottom layer of stones was placed so that the second layer of stones could sit on top of them, and the top stone was placed on the second layer.

Every landmark, boundaries, and walls had their own separate set of pylons. You have three categories: 5-circle representing how you relate/ the 4-circle boundaries for the five relationships/ and the pylons that determine your boundaries.

In Genesis 2–3, God told Adam and Eve to be fruitful and multiply. In Genesis 6, God told Noah and his family to multiply and fill the earth. In Genesis 11, God saw the tower that men were building to keep them from filling the earth. The tower was made with fired bricks of clay, and tar from the nearby tar fields of the mud plain of Shinar stuck the bricks together. What was the purpose for them building a tower? I found two: one was to keep people from scattering over the earth and filling it, and the other was to unite humankind in common, leaving God out of their lives. They planned to be self-sufficient. These two purposes have passed down through the generations to ensure people's independence from God. The way they lived showed how depraved their thinking became.

The story of the pre-flood days of Noah was similar, and even going back to the downfall of Adam and Eve, when self-thinking and being independent were their goals. They were not much different from us in modern times, having the same frame of mind. It's what human nature is like when no one remembers God.

In the Sermon on the Mount Jesus said that the kingdom of God was within the believer's heart. Our heart consists of three parts representing the tabernacle: the outer court, the inner court, and the holy of holies. Our interaction with God through prayer and worship takes place in the most holy place, the inner court represents the cleansing and fellowship with God through the blood of Jesus, and the outer court is where we bring our sacrifices to God. These spiritual walls are as important as our emotional walls. Christ is our foundation, our cornerstone. These are bricks made by God, not by men.

When people use their human-made bricks to build walls, they must hold them together with cement. Jesus is the one holding together the spiritual temple in which God dwells. Nothing human-made, used, or needed. The Bible tells us that God uses each believer as building stones for building His church, the bride of Christ.

In God's eyes, all humanity is in the same boat: outside His light. When a person turns to God in repentance of his sins, God adopts that person into His family and looks at them through the cleansing blood of Jesus on the cross. Those in the family of God are using God's bricks of love and its nine fruits to construct relationships. When we come together to worship God in a public place, we build each other up. We are light to them, and they are light to us.

Regarding nonbelievers, each one is darkness to another. Their deeds show that they are filled with dark thoughts. They despise being around believers because they cannot stand the light of God shining from the believer. They continue to center their rebellion against Him, and they build their tower consisting of self-made bricks.

Therefore, there are two purposes for building walls. One is to keep ourselves safe from others reaching us, and the other is to keep us from reaching out to others. We might ask ourselves, Which side am I on, the inside or the outside?

God's Word, the Bible, is our instruction book for living. We read to learn of God and His purpose for humankind. His purpose is for us to know Him and have a personal relationship with Him. He promises to make our hearts His residence. Our highest responsibility is to give God glory in all things we do or say.

Boundaries help me identify what belongs to me and what belongs to others. There are three categories: landmarks, boundaries, and walls. These three categories apply to individuals—everything we own—and our relationships to others, what we do, think, and feel. Boundaries are every-where and necessary. Our skin is the body's boundary that keeps us intact and prevents foreign objects that may harm us from entering. Our homes and property keep us separate from our neighbors. Our religion keeps us separate from those who do not believe as we do. Our work has boundaries set to indicate when and how we complete our work. Our social life has guidelines that identify our group from another group. Our relationships have boundaries and define what we do together, when, where, and why.

Review of the pylons:

In Old Testament times, the Jewish people placed stones, called pylons, at the corners of their property. The bottom pile had three stones, then two stones placed on them, and one stone stacked on top of the two. These py-lons marked your boundaries, and without them, confusion and enmesh-ment could quickly occur. Sometimes an enemy would scatter or remove the pylons, hoping to steal part of the land.

While pylons keep you safe on your land, emotional boundaries keep you safe and assist you in building healthy relationships. Emotional boundaries were set in your heart and mind by significant others in your early childhood, e.g., parents and siblings. If instead you received rejection, abandonment, or were abused physically, sexually, emotionally, or intellec-tually, the moving boundaries left you without clear guidelines as to who you are, leaving you an emotional wreck. Healthy emotional boundaries create confidence to face life with success.

So far, we have learned there are five boundaries, and each one of those has its set of four rings. Each of the four rings has its set of pylons—either a Faith pylon or a Fear pylon. Healthy boundaries are Faith pylons, and unhealthy boundaries are Fear pylons.

The bottom layer of stones is either the Fruit of the Spirit or the Works of the flesh.

The top stone represents your healthy pylon called Faith. The other top stone represents your moved pylon called Fear. The middle stones represent the four assurances: Acceptance, Security, Safety, Space, and Place in the healthy pylon called Faith.

In the moved pylon called Fear, the middle stones represent the five underlying fears: Rejection, Abandonment, Pain, Engulfment, and Fear of Fear.

The bottom layer represents the Fruit of the Spirit in the healthy pylon: Love, Joy, Peace, Long-suffering, Kindness, Goodness, Faithfulness, Gentleness, Self-control.

Stress scattered the marked boundaries. Now it rains and puddles form, revealing the dents in the ground where the original stones were. Instead of rainwater, imagine the puddles are filled with gasoline. Your feelings become a landmine. Everybody has some of these fears, but some take on more.

Our purpose is to get the fear-like tangles out of our lives.

Each one of these four categories have either their faith or their fear factors. Our pylon has three layers in the shape of a pyramid. The top represents faith or fear; the middle represents either assurances or the five underlying causes of fear; the bottom represents either the fruit of the Spirit or the works of the flesh.

Healthy boundaries are in place.

F = Finding my inner child requires me to

A = Align my belief system

I   = Involves changing all my false beliefs into

T = Truth statements that are supported by Scripture

H = Healthy boundaries and a healthy inner child will be
       the result of doing this.

Four Assurances

1. Acceptance

2. Security

3. Safety and Healing

4. Space and a Place

Moved boundaries are not healthy.

F = Fear is the opposite of faith

E = Emptying all my fear and replacing it with faith

A = Allows me to acquire healthy boundaries to

R = Reparent my inner child

Five basic fears:

1. Rejection

2. Abandonment

3. Pain

4. Engulfment

5. Fear of Fear

Shame says you are a mistake; something is wrong with you. It is not just a feeling.

Least intense:

Irritation

Frustration

Anxiety

Fear > depression

Shame (most intense)

If your reaction to something is more significant than it ought to be, then you have touched something deeper.

Dr. Sydney: Here are two poems about faith and fear. Jerry, will you read these aloud?

Jerry: "What Faith Has Done for Me"

"Faith is expecting something good to happen, and it does and is the opposite of fear. When faith is present, there is no room for fear. It removes rejection and gives me acceptance, and it removes abandonment and gives me the assurance I am wanted. Faith removes the fear of unwanted experiences repeating and gives me competence and self-assurance. It removes engulfment, gives me personal space, and removes the unknown's fear, and gives me hope for the future.[55]

The next one is Fear Is Just Like a Dream[56]

FEAR IS JUST LIKE A DREAM

Nightmares come to us in our dreams.
We wake up, and the dream disappears.
Fears come to us in our delusions.
And when we confront them with reality,
Like nightmares do, fears disappear.
We meet our fear in dream-like fantasies
It dissolves upon awakening not to bother us again.

All that we are afraid of is delusional
And lacks common sense.
Something we perceive as a lack of a
Dissatisfaction with ourselves or others.
So, fear attaches to that delusion and
Steals our peace, calmness, and sound mind.

Just as in the nightmare, all the fear, anger,
and suffering we experience comes from
not realizing that we are only daydreaming,
So, all the fear and suffering we experience comes
from not seeing the fundamental nature of our world.

Common sense and experience guard our lives.
More often than not, we do not use common sense.

> Appearances entirely fool us,
> not for a moment do we question their validity.
>
> If we did question appearances, we would discover
> that is all they are: mere appearances to mind,
> with no real object behind them.
> The enemy we fight or flee from is no more accurate
> than the tiger in the dream and has no more power
> to harm what we are. So, wake up.

"Fear flees away from faith as darkness flees away from light. Lord, fill my heart with faith, so it is completely overflowing, and there is no room for anything else."

Infantile Fears	Translated As	Extended Feeling	Adult Issues
Loud, unexpected noises	Danger, alarm, warning of an attack	The threat of harm or death	Rejection
Falling	Dropped, turned loose, disconnected	Left alone, discarded, forsaken	Abandonment
Tight restraint	Controlled, loss of freedom, overwhelmed, "eaten."	Smothered, absorbed, loss of identity	Engulfment
1. Rejection		Needs warm, kind words	
2. Abandonment		Needs friendly, loving touching	
3. Pain memory — whatever you experienced that you do not want to experience again		Needs safety, evidence of acceptance, nonverbal language, not words	
4. Engulfment		Needs space and a place	
The resulting concept of God as a therapist or rapist			
5. Fear of Fear itself (the unknown, the future), the feeling of being "raped" is this kind of fear or fear feeling		Needs unconditional love, acceptance	

Session 17—Who I Am—My Personal Inventory

"Who I Am" Inventory

Representation of My Outer Self

1. I am a Christian.

2. I enjoy traveling.

3. I love Jesus with my whole heart.

4. I am a good cook.

5. I enjoy doing Bible study.

6. I have the gift of calming people.

7. I enjoy watercolor painting.

8. I enjoy writing poetry.

9. I enjoy counseling.

10. I enjoy my family.

11. I enjoy listening to and talking with the elderly.

JERRY: Jan surprised me on my birthday with a party and invited my friends over. She wrote a beautiful letter and decorated the house. From the ceiling fan were hung many red hearts with words of affirmation on them. These were written on the hearts:

You are a man of faith, you are a peacemaker, you have goals, you are loving, you are saved, you are long-suffering, you are cherished, you are a good listener, you are a man of integrity, you are kind, you are a victor, you are gracious, you have strong faith, you are a companion, you are my valentine, you are wise, you are a deep thinker, you are My beloved son, you are a believer, you are a father, you are grateful, you are a good cook, you are a man, you are a loved brother, you are a counselor, you are trustworthy, you are a friend, you are redeemed, you are dependable, you are a husband, you are generous, you are a mighty warrior, you are an artist, you are patient, you are honest, you are truthful, you are a Christ-follower, you have character, you are handsome, you are merciful, you are a gentleman.

In addition, I have had the loving support of my wife, Jan throughout my search to figuring out who I am. She wrote this significant letter to me:

Jerry, God showed me how you have been shaped and clothed with the false/counterfeit since infancy that is now being traded for the new/true. God showed me how you put on the identity of Wycliffe and spent years on the mission field, and that was the good that you chose. Now you have been stripped, and there seems to be no you. All of who you have been burned, for our God is a consuming fire. It is out of the fire and out of the furnace that the phoenix rises, and how Daniel became refined, purified with gold, silver, and precious stones remaining.

Even as Lazarus died, he was in the tomb for four days before he came alive again. Know, man of God, He will not leave you in the fire to perish. He will not leave you in the furnace to burn. He will not leave you in this grave, but at just the right time, He will say to you, "Jerry, come forth," and your grave clothes will be taken off. And you will indeed go forth in power and authority to do the work you have been designed to do from before the foundation of time. Luv ya!

"We are God's handiwork, created in Christ Jesus to do good works, which God prepared in advance for us to do" (Ephesians 2:10 KJV).

Jerry, here is a word to encourage you today. "On that day, I will raise the fallen booth of David, and wall up its breaches; I will also raise its ruins and rebuild it as in the days of old" (Amos 9:11).

My Dreams Are Yours

Whatever dreams I ever have, however old or new, they are the pictures and thoughts I want to share with you. The plans I have for everything I hope will come my way, and all the magic beauty that belongs to yesterday. I want to take them in my hand and bring them to your door and promise you that all of them are yours always. I want your heart to understand that every dream in me is one that you will inspire with your love, loyalty, and so whatever dreams I have, whether old or new, I sincerely want to say they all belong to you.

"The thief comes only to steal and kill and destroy. I came that they may have life and have it abundantly" (John 10:10).

Dr. Sydney, now let us check the "Me" survey.

Jerry: My hobbies are Bible study, photography, poetry, reading, watercolor, movies, sightseeing/traveling, and working with the elderly.

Here are some of my poems:

The Cry of My Soul

"O, Lord, my God, the cry of my soul is for as much of you as I can hold. Empty me of all that's not from you so I can love you with all my heart, so I can love you with all my soul, so I can love you with all my mind. You are my heart's desire, and I want to worship you.

"My heart thirsts for you more than the deer thirsts for the water brook in a dry land. You are the one who satisfies my longings. All others are counterfeit and leave me wanting. You are my heart's desire. I desire no other, for only you can satisfy."

Jesus Is Awesome

When we are where God wants us to be, huge, terrifying storms may come, but Jesus is there just at the right time to assure us and let us get a glimpse of His great glory and power. Jesus did not come quickly to the disciples. He knew the storm was raging, and He knew the disciples were in trouble, but He waited and delayed His coming.

We may have been in the storm too long and wonder, where is Jesus? Why isn't He here? But Jesus delayed His coming to the disciples so that, like them, we would experience His great power and glory over nature. When their natural strength was gone, Jesus came just at the time He knew the conditions were right for a miracle.

He spoke to the disciples amid the storm. "It is all right," he said. "I am here! Do not be afraid."

We may be longing to hear these words from Jesus. Life has gone crazy, and we are in the middle of the worst situation one could imagine, but even in the darkest hour of the night, when there was no hope, Jesus comes walking on the surface of those stormy waves, those waves that cause us to fear, and speaks reassuring words of comfort to us. "It is okay. I am here. Do not be afraid."

When this happens, we exclaim, "You are the Son of God."

What Does Praying Mean to Me?

I believe praying means having a heart-to-heart talk with God.

I believe praying is being amazed at God's glory.

I believe praying is talking with God, having no particular schedule.

I believe praying is meditating on God's Word.

I believe praying is repeating Scriptures back to God.

I believe praying is being alert to God's presence with me.

I believe praying is the believers' weapon against Satan.

I believe praying is waiting on God to speak to me.

I believe praying is humbly yielding my thoughts to God.

I believe praying is offering my body, soul, and spirit to God.

I believe praying is singing hymns and songs to God.

I believe praying is obedience to God.

I believe praying is expressing my deepest hurts and sorrows to God.

I believe praying can be expressed in groanings that I do not know how to put into words.

I believe praying is Holy Communion with God.

I believe praying is telling God "I love you."

I believe praying is writing in your journal and willingly letting God read it.

I believe praying is not using a set of rituals to gain God's favor.

I believe praying is not presenting my wish list to God of things I want.

I believe praying is not demanding God do this or that.

Prayer is the nearest approach that, in our present state, we can make to deity. To neglect or shun this duty is to shun all approaches to God.

THE STRONGER THE TRIALS

The stronger the trials the harder I lean into God. The chaos and storms of life rage. They drive me deeper into the arms of God. I have no fear whatever may come. The storms of life came to test my obedience to God. I know God knows what is happening to me.

Pain and suffering will try my faith. My anchor holds in spite of the test. I stay close to God through prayer and His word. My life is in God, and He is in control. Nothing touches me without His consent. He knows my faith will stand true. God honors me with life's woes for I am in His arms, and He will never let go. He whispers love and comfort as I rest in peace. Pain and suffering cannot control my heart though they try. I am stayed upon God's embrace. My response, "Not my will, but yours be done." I bow in worship as your Spirit flows into the depths of my heart and this I know. Your presence my assurance as I journey with you, I can face the world when I lean into you.

I visualize heaven this way. John is looking up to heaven and sees a door standing open. I tried to picture what John saw.

BEFORE THE THRONE OF GOD

God gave me beautiful people of faith into my life when I needed encouragement. My Bible Study teacher Sylvia Engle gave me this word of prophecy in 1996. When I get discouraged I read this. I visualize this is something God could say to me.

Jerry, My Son,

Know once and for all, and for all time my Word, my promises, my inheritance reserved for you stand true for all time for you.

Come, sit at my feet, ask me, and I will give you understanding, Seek my face, and I will smile on you.

And I fill your soul with peace and gladness. Knock, and I will open the door of my kingdom wide to you, and you shall dwell there with me. I am your heavenly Father who gives the gift of the Holy Spirit to you.

Do not fear, do not be afraid. For I am the Lord Your God, and I am with you. I knew you in your Mother's womb and interwove you there. You are fearfully and wonderfully made.

You are my artistry; I am the One who has searched you and known you. I know when you sit and stand. I understand your every thought and your every path when you lie down and get up.

I know all your ways. I knew all your words altogether. I have hedged you in front and behind and laid my hand on you. There is nowhere you can go to get away from my spirit, from my presence. I lead you with my hand, I hold you with my right hand. When you thought you were hidden in the darkness, I saw you. Indeed, both darkness and light are the same to me.

My Son, let your mind no longer be unstable. Let me settle you. Come to the place where every doubt is crucified on the cross and you instead choose to trust me, in all things.

It is your choice and your decision, and I do not change. I am the same yesterday, today, and tomorrow. Come and take your place at my table. I have plans for you.

There is none like you in all my kingdom, and I desire much that the fruit I have prepared for you be brought to harvest. Come with me, my beloved Son.

You have thought I am too broken, too far back, too wounded. I invite you to see yourself as I see you. Lay aside the old ways of looking at yourself. Trust that I am the healer of your soul. Rise in courage and boldness out of that place of fear and insecurity. Fear is not of Me. Insecurity is not the habitation I have for you.

I see you as a child, Jerry, walking around in your Father's boots. They are huge, and it seems like you could never grow into them, but I tell you truly you are growing even now, and the boots, even combat boots, are ready for you to put on. Trust. Believe. Obey.

Heavenly Father, my heart desires to live a holy life that honors you as my welcome guest. You know all about me. There are places where impure thoughts are hiding. Search my heart for the negative thoughts hiding there and reveal them to me. Please give me the strength to capture these and expose them for what they are. They cannot hide anymore. Shine forth, O Lord, with your light that destroys whatever is not pleasing to you. Please help me in my weakness when new deceiving thoughts tempt me to turn from you. I long to be the man you see me be. Thank you in the name of Jesus. Amen.

CHAPTER 7

SESSIONS 18–22

Celebration

SESSION 18—FAMILY UPDATE

DR. SYDNEY: Good day, Jerry. There is a bottle of cold water on the table for you. Let us pray. Heavenly Father, I am claiming Philippians 1:6, that you will continue the excellent work you have begun in Jerry's life. Lord, help him understand the concept I am teaching and have wisdom in applying it to his daily life. Bless him with your peace this morning. In the name of Jesus, I pray. Amen.

Jerry, please bring me up to date with your family, especially Steve.

JERRY: I am going to pretend I can read Steve's thoughts. Basically, by his actions, Steve asked two questions: Can I have my way? and Am I loved?

The answer to the first question is yes. Steve probably felt abandoned and lonely and thought we did not care enough to discipline him. Steve may have felt he did not have our love. We found it easier to do things ourselves rather than let Steve do them. But we wanted Steve to see that we did love him, so we established boundaries and followed through with them, despite his testing of us. We demonstrated our love through a different mood and mind-frame than Steve had seen before. Steve may have disrespected himself for getting away with not obeying us.

Steve, you are wanted and greatly loved, and you are an essential part of our family.

To Rescue or Not to Rescue

We do love Steve and care very much about what happens to him. We made lots of mistakes in our relationship with Steve, but now we are correcting those.

159

Steve found out the hard way that we had changed when he ran away from HeartLight early in 1993. He ran away, and HeartLight told him he could not come back. We also told him he could not come home. We told him we loved him too much to let him have his way, and that he was not ready to come home. He still had a bad attitude and had not worked through his problems. If he came home just then, things would drift back to the old patterns of relating that neither of us wanted.

In the past, if this type of thing happened, we would have rescued him, but this time we did not. Steve had to swallow his pride and go back to HeartLight and apologize to the staff and earn the privilege of living there again, which he did. He also realized we had changed. Later, when Steve did return home, the whole family met and came up with guidelines of what was acceptable and what was not. Steve settled into our home, and we loved having him with us again.

The first five years of Steve's life were happy. Jan and I read books to him, made playdough, and played Legos with him. He loved art and had a natural talent for drawing. He spoke three languages fluently (Weri, Pidgin, and English), loved wildlife, and knew the different spiders, birds, and animals. Steve had many different pet animals that we took back and forth with us when we went to the village. He knew the Weri culture and mixed some things up. In Weri, a person shows anger by spitting on the ground. That does not go well in the USA inside a stranger's home that we overnighted with when traveling!

Steve was well-behaved up to six years old. When he started 1st-grade, the teacher noticed Steve needed glasses. We had his eyes tested and yes, he had a lazy eye. He hated wearing the glasses. He became disruptive at school and rebellious at home. On hind-sight, I believe he started have problems with ADHD at this time. We had no way to test him. He hated school and was bored quickly. His mind was very active, thinking about the things he loved, and he could hardly wait for school to finish for the day so he could play. We did not know it, but he had Attention Deficit Hyperactivity Disorder (ADHD). He had behavior problems, such as difficulty attending to instruction, focusing on schoolwork, keeping up with assignments, following instructions, completing tasks, and social interactions. I misunderstood him and thought he was deliberately choosing to disobey. At this point, we could not trust him to do something we asked him to do. Instead of getting mad at him all the time, I found it easier to do things myself rather than asking him and him not doing it. He saw me as a bully and angry with him, and I saw him as rebellious.

Jan was sick, so I took care of Steve most of the time, with some Weri teenage girls, Pitia, Ariate, and Tu'pe. We were in the village for five straight months. At that point Steve enjoyed life. One of the Weri practices was to trick people: deception, and I did not know if Steve was following the Weri way of thinking or not.

Our Wycliffe doctor told Jan her problems were mental and for us to go home and see a psychologist, so we did. We had to take emergency sick leave for Jan to receive treatment in her home country, New Zealand. Steve was four and a half years old. In New Zealand, the psychologist told Jan her problems were physical and recommended a doctor who had been in Papua New Guinea and now had a private practice in Auckland, where we were staying. Jan's blood tests showed her to be a walking zoo: Brucellosis, giardia, hookworm, and malaria. No wonder she was depressed and ill.

Jan had extreme depression and was sick from the time Steve was two and a half until he started kindergarten. I had a good relationship with Steve and looked after him all that time. When Jan began feeling better, she started to have more to do with Steve. Her way of relating to him was different from mine. Since Jan was feeling better, I went to work at the WBT New Zealand office. Steve resented me for not being there for him as before.

When Steve was eight years old, we had a baby girl, Wendy. Most of our attention then went to Wendy, and Steve reacted negatively to his baby sister. Since he did not get the attention he wanted, he acted out.

Had anything changed about us that he could see? We still focused on outside things, but Steve probably wanted us to focus more on him. He saw the concerned parents' activities, but he may have been so frustrated and angry at not finding what he desired from us that he thought we loved work and activities more than him. He saw no value in our work, only that it robbed him of our time and love. In Papua New Guinea, Steve trashed our home, symbolic of his hate for the mission and being a missionary kid. He would not talk to us about New Guinea and how he was feeling.

The main thing is, he is now living a healthy lifestyle and raising his son with love and care. God restored each one of us and is now blessing us in ways we never dreamed.

Our Trip Back to PNG

Jan, Wendy, and I made a trip back to Papua New Guinea for a month to pack up and say goodbye to everything left undone and for emotional closure. We went to Tauta for a week, where we received a royal welcome. Most things looked the same as they did when I left in 1991. Our cat, Spice, was thrilled to see us.

Later, I went into the literacy office and looked around. I saw all those stencils I worked so hard on that last week in the village still lying there, not printed. I was deeply hurt. I realized things important to me were not vital to them. I don't know what they used as a substitute for those stories on the stencils. I didn't bother to ask. I kept thinking to myself, Did I waste those three years working so hard for nothing? Later, back at the main base, I realized all that work was for the wrong motive anyway.

The Lord broke my heart, and I had to commit myself and the Rawa literacy to Him. I also had to commit my family to Him because I almost lost them in doing the literacy project for the Rawas.

I was afraid of God, and I was afraid of myself. All I knew about God had been shaken to my core. What I knew about me scared me almost to death. I believed God had turned His back on me, and I hated myself enough that suicidal thoughts were my comfort. My family and I desperately needed help mentally, physically, and emotionally.

Many of our friends and supporting churches did not know what to do with us. My home church had its problems and did not know how to help us. We were stuck in the middle. It hurt too much to stay stuck, and it hurt to move forward. During the darkest hours, God led us to Little Flock Ministries. At Little Flock, we were surrounded by hurting people who found new life and hope for a better tomorrow.

We listened and worked with Dr. Gilliam one week at a time. God showed up and worked miracles in our lives. Finally, after four years of intense counseling and yielding to God, He let us return to Papua New Guinea for one month. Friends looked after Steve while Wendy, Jan, and I went back. As we sorted the stuff in storage, we wondered why most of it had seemed essential to keep. We did not send home much that was there. We said goodbye to friends and felt ready to come back to the States.

On February 8, 1995, just as the sun was rising, I went outside the house in Papua New Guinea to find some memory rocks. I chose a handful and wrote "goodbye" on them, one for each thing I wanted to be rid of. Then I piled them all in one area on the grass and took a photo. Just then I found a grubworm at the bottom of the pile. Its head was sticking about a half-inch above ground. It was looking straight up at me. What a surprise! In its struggle to get above ground, see the sunshine, and breathe the fresh morning air, it ran straight into a pile of heavy rocks which kept the sunshine and fresh air from it.

I took the rocks to the nearby river and threw them into the water. Just as I thought these heavy burdens, dead dreams, happy and sad memories would crush us, Jesus lifted all those burdens, and none of them could come back to block my way.

After throwing the rocks in the river, it was as if I, too, was like that little worm, holding my head up high and saying thanks for taking away those heavy burdens. I departed Papua New Guinea sad yet excited about the new day starting in our lives. I didn't know what I was ahead, but at least didn't have those old rocks weighing me down.

❦

I had been living under the mistaken idea that since I was in full-time service for Him, God would spare me from the turmoil of life. But God was more concerned for my relationship with Him than my work for Him. He had a lot to teach me, and He allowed circumstances in my life to show me what my heart was like. God said, "I am the Lord, and there is no other." What scares me more than facing evil head-on is facing the living God head-on when I am out of fellowship with Him. He is love. He is also a consuming fire.

This is what God said about King Cyrus: "I am the Lord, and there is no other; besides Me, there is no God. I will gird you, though you have not known Me; that men may know from the rising to the setting of the sun that there is no one besides Me. I am the Lord, and there is no other. The One forming light and creating darkness, causing wellbeing, and creating calamity; I am the Lord who does all these" (Isaiah 45:5–7).

"The one who practices sin is of the devil, for the devil has sinned from the beginning. The Son of God appeared for this purpose, to destroy the works of the devil" (1 John 3:8).

Back in Dallas, I continued receiving therapy and assisting in ministry at Little Flock with Dr. Gilliam.

Session 19—Memory Markers

Dr. Sydney: Good morning, Jerry. Let us pray. Dear Lord, thank you for allowing me to work with Jerry. I thank you for the progress he has made, and I pray you will continue to work in his life. In Jesus's name, amen.

Today I want to show you how to celebrate the great things God has done for you since we began counseling. We want something unique and meaningful for you to look back on for the rest of your life.

How to Design a Memory Marker

Now I will teach you to celebrate all the deep, cleansing work God has done in your life. We will make a memory marker for each place you want to call holy ground, and upright stones of remembrance like Abraham, Isaac, and Jacob did. When you see this memory marker, you will think of the work God did in your life.

Remember, a memory marker is like a signpost on the highway telling you something is ahead that is meaningful to you, a memorial of God doing work in your life that you can celebrate each time you pass that way. In what areas has God done a work that drastically impacted you? Find that, and you will have a victory worth celebrating. It is holy ground!

Jerry: Oh, I understand. It is a story picture to illustrate how some things in my life tried to trip me up, but with God's help, those places turned into steppingstones instead of obstacles. They are now cleansed and holy.

Dr. Sydney: An emotional marker is a picture to remember a significant event. Examples of events you might want to remember:

*making a crucial decision that affects you or others (exchange of wedding rings)

*correction of a false belief (Deborah's baby shoes and verses written and framed, regarding weeping)

An emotional marker can be significant in several ways: because it is unique to you; because it is associated with a person or place; because of the season; because it is something you did or did not do. (Deborah climbed a tree because it was something Little Debbie did.)

An emotional marker needs to involve something physical. Involve as many senses as possible.

A memory marker requires some (but not a lot) of creativity. To those who claim to have none, remember, you are made in the image of God, and He is the creator.

Examples of emotional markers:

Pages of your journal bound to a rock and tossed in a river, representing breaking ties to the past.

Write a letter to whoever offended you. It does not have to be mailed.

A photograph dated and labeled with the significance of the photo.

A dump truck filled with the horror of the past but decorated with God's promises for the future.

Brick turned to dust by D & D Demolitions, with God's promise of recovery attached.

Cross of flowers representing the time of forgiveness made possible only because of Christ's death on the cross.

Dalmatian puppies (accept the blots of life as God's gift in developing Christ's likeness).

Flowers for a grave placed on brick from the house where the abuse happened—each flower chosen for its meaning.

We will begin reviewing the care plan and will continue in our next session. Here is a copy for you. I want to know if you understand the process of reparenting the inner child and landmarks, boundaries, and walls.

The areas you are unclear on, we will schedule another session to go over that area. You will need to know all these steps, because some things may come up that you will need to process. When that happens, you will have the skills to do the work yourself to reparent Little Jerry Wayne to align your beliefs with Scripture.

Our last session will be in three weeks unless you have something else you want to process.

DR. SYDNEY: Hello, Jerry. If you are thirsty, there is a bottle of cold water on the table for you. Let us pray. Lord, it is hard to believe these sessions with Jerry will soon be over. I have seen tremendous changes in his life, and I give you thanks for working so wonderfully in him. You took a scared, little dark pony and transformed him into a mighty warhorse for your kingdom. Bless our time together today. Amen.

In three weeks, on the 30th, please bring guests with you for your presentation. My staff will be present, and we will have refreshments at 9:00, and your presentation will begin at 9:30. Please phone the office and tell the receptionist how many are coming.

Today we will continue our review to work on your negative self-talk and replace it with positive self-talk; to work on your belief system; to work on the lies you have believed; to work on ways to reparent Little Jerry Wayne; to work on helping him grow up.

I will also introduce landmarks, boundaries, and walls, which will need to be set and reset to work on patterns for living; to identify the different boundaries; to determine the components of each boundary; and finally, design a memory marker.

DR. SYDNEY: Heavenly Father, you are amazing. You have transformed Jerry into a wonderful man of God, one who seeks after your heart with passion and courage. Thank you for the privilege of being part of this process. My heart is full of praise to you for the great things you have done in restoring Jerry to the mighty warrior he is today. I am proud to call him my brother. In the name of Jesus, all blessing and honor and power be to His holy name. Amen.

We are going to the mall and lunch. We will look for something you can use to design your memory markers that highlights the victory you have over the past. Our last official counseling session will be next week. If you have more thoughts on memory markers, I will be proud to see these. After we eat, I will meet you at the main entrance at 1:00. Here is a twenty-dollar bill to buy whatever you need for designing your memory marker. The sessions we have on memory markers are complimentary. You may invite guests. If you need more time, that will be fine. We will be in the Board Room for your presentation.

Session 20—Presentation of Victory Markers

Dr. Sydney: Jerry, good morning. Let us pray. Heavenly Father, this counseling journey is coming to an end. Just look at Jerry, your son. When we first started this process, Jerry was hurting and not sure what would happen. You did your work in his life, and he is a happy, healthy man. I am so proud of Jerry. Thank you for changing him into this mighty warrior for you. You have brought healing to Steve. Thank you for the lovely, sweet Wendy, and for working in her life. Lord, you have been wonderful to Jan, healing her and bearing with her in this emotional journey with Jerry. All praise to you. Amen.

Welcome, everyone. Today, we are celebrating with Jerry. He is sharing his victory markers for places in his life where God did a deep cleansing in critical places.

I can hardly wait for you to present your victory markers. Jerry selected key places and designed something unique to remind him that God was faithful. In the Old Testament, Abraham, Isaac, Jacob, and Samuel selected a pile of stones to mark the spot for something unique.

Jerry: My first one is crabgrass and the praying mantis.

One Saturday morning, I awoke feeling restless. I thought about my counselor and the unsettling discoveries of how I related to others, and I was frightened. I needed to do something to get rid of my stress. Therefore, I went outside to the front yard and started pulling up the crabgrass that was growing. I linked the crabgrass with the bitterness that ruled my life.

I was so angry that I pulled up enough crabgrass to fill two large-sized yard-waste bags. It worked; the stress was relieved. There was still a lot of crabgrass to pull up if ever I got stressed again. Crabgrass is that horrible weed that will take over a yard if it is not removed. The removal of the crabgrass helped me focus on my attitude about the abuse.

Three mornings in a row, there was a praying mantis either on my car's windshield or hood. The third time I saw it, I looked hard at the praying mantis because it was directly in front of my face on the windshield. That night in my sleep, I was troubled, and I tossed and turned much of the night.

Crabgrass and bitterness know no boundaries; they cannot be easily removed, and you must pull them up by their roots. Otherwise, they spread quickly by sending out new runners and suckers to take control. These easily take root and send out more of their kind. When the gardener removes the unwanted crabgrass, if he leaves even a part of the root, it grows again, ready to take over the whole area.

The praying mantis is a deceitful insect that eats other insects. It pretends it is a flower or innocent saintly being when it is waiting for its next meal. The praying mantis and the abuser pretend to be something they are not; they attack the unsuspecting. The female mantis even eats the male's head when they are mating—a fitting picture of what happened to me.

A gardener cares for a garden or yard, similar to my caring counselor and friend. He is the only person I have ever allowed to search my deepest secrets. He sees the skeletons of my childhood ruined by my praying-mantis abusers. Can I trust him to be gentle and supporting as the crabgrass is pulled up?

These are the main off-shoots of the original root of sexual abuse as I perceive them:

1. Unhealthy and unnatural appetite for sex with others or self.

2. Suspicion of family, friends, and children close to me.

3. Hatred of self, father, God, and family.

4. Indecisiveness in choosing friends, work, family, and spending money.

5. Negative thinking of self and relations with others in self-image, self-esteem, feelings, happiness, sex, food, work, family relations, and impure thoughts.

Bitterness, anger, greed, impure thoughts and actions, and a long list of other emotions take deep root in my heart. Before I know it, I have many unwanted roots that rob me from freely interacting with those around me. I superimpose my bitterness, anger, greed, impure thoughts, and actions on those I love or hate, which feeds more runners and suckers to grow. Jesus is the only gardener I know who can altogether remove all the roots and suckers from my heart. My crabgrass emotions have feelings and hurt when the gardener cuts away their roots, but pain and suffering are needful for a time to teach me not to allow other crabgrass to grow.

2. The Turkey and The Eagle

God looks at us as eagles, but we look at ourselves as turkeys. Turkeys can fly, but not very well. We are like the turkey hanging onto all our past garbage, clinging to it with bungee cords, holding us back when we try to fly. We take off and then are slammed down to the ground because of the attached cords to that past baggage. I started thinking about the garbage in my life. Throw out the trash. Let the garbage truck take it off to the dump, never to be seen again.

I wanted to get a toy garbage truck, but I couldn't find one anywhere. I didn't want a matchbox size for what I planned to do. Later Jan and Wendy found just the right one in a shop, and they bought it for me. I printed off a set of my journal notes and took these to the photocopier, reducing them so they would all fit on two pieces of paper. I wadded them up and put them inside the garbage truck.

Then I saw a pair of turkey earrings and bought them. At the same time, I found this beautiful eagle with its wings spread like it was taking off for flight. I had a fishhook tie-tack and used that for the hook, and I attached a rubber band to it and around the turkey's legs. I then attached the hook and the turkey to the back of the garbage truck. I put the eagle on top, and then wrote various Scriptures on labels and stuck them on the top, sides, and bottom of the truck.

When I finished, I had a lovely, meaningful reminder of the eagle passage in Isaiah 40:28–31 and the things I learned from Dr. Gilliam. "Do you not know? Have you not heard? The Everlasting God, the LORD, the Creator of the ends of the earth does not become weary or tired. His understanding is unsearchable. He gives strength to the weary, and to the one who lacks might, He increases power. Though youths grow weary and tired, and vigorous young men stumble badly, yet those who wait for the LORD will gain new strength; they will mount up with wings like eagles, they will run and not get tired, they will walk and not become weary."

God says to me, "You are an eagle."

I say I am a turkey. Eagles can soar and fly high even in the storm. The turkey can fly up to roost on a tree branch.

God says, "I have taken away your sins and made them white as snow."

I say I am stuck in sin, and there is no way out. I am a turkey; that is me.

God says, "I have set you free."

The turkey says, "I can fly. Sin pulls me back like a bungee cord that is attached to my leg."

God says, "Give me all your junk."

The turkey says, "Without God, I am good for nothing."

God says, "I have been waiting for you to humble yourself; I have changed your heart. You belong to me."

The turkey says, "Thank you for giving me my identity. I am an eagle and not the turkey I thought me to be."

Dr. Sydney: Thank you so much. This next session will be our last unless you have something you want to process. See you next week.

Session 21—Continued Victory Markers

Jerry: I have more thoughts on other memory markers I want to share with you.

Parables of My Life

I am in a flower garden, and I see some of the flowers wilting. I water the flowers and loosen the ground around each. I pull the weeds and make the garden beautiful like it once was. I prop up the flowers that have fallen over.

I am a beautiful rose. As the sun moves across the sky, I follow it with my face, always facing up and turning as the sun moves from morning to evening. I keep my face looking toward the sun.

I am standing on the other side of a high brick wall that I built. Jesus is there with me, and we need to break down that wall. Jesus asks me to hand him the bricks one at a time as we take that wall down. I name each clay brick as I hand it to Him: the clay brick of lack of faith, the slab of fear, the chunk of anger. As I give Him each brick, the glory of God shines through the place where the block was until the wall is gone, and Jesus and I are standing in the open, surrounded by the glory of God.

I am walking in a very dark valley, and Jesus is walking beside me. We are laughing and talking and enjoying ourselves. We come to a tunnel, and I hesitate to continue. Jesus reassures me that He is with me. Psalm 23:4, paraphrased: I will fear no evil for you are with me.

I enter the tunnel, and we see a bright light at the end. Jesus tells me it is not a train and that I just need to trust Him because something beautiful awaits us on the other side.

Dr. Sydney: You have a powerful imagination. May you bless others with your word pictures, poems, writings, and Bible study. Jerry, it is my pleasure to watch you grow healthy.

Jerry: Thank you.

The Old Wooden Plank

I took you from the house now lying in a heap. You are still in excellent condition and shine like new. The secrets you hid for so long are now exposed. Good and evil were there so long ago. God worked a deep cleansing of the sexual abuse that occurred. I will make a memory marker out of you, old wooden plank.

I selected this plank from the pile because it showed no aging and shined like new. You will remind me of God's abundant grace. I am branding you with a hot soldering iron. The letters I choose are from an old gospel song. "No one ever cared for me like Jesus; there is no other friend so kind as He." Now you have a place of honor in my life.

Teddy Bear Jerry Wayne

I have never known anyone like you. You have that sly grin and dancing eyes. You stand up tall, and I feel proud when I see you. You are so handsome and dressed up nicely. You are even wearing shoes that fit your feet. You have lovely blue trousers and a red shirt. Around your neck, you wear a gold medal. Even without the first-place decoration, you are a winner for me. I love you, teddy bear Jerry Wayne.

Lost Identity

When it came time to share something about my life with others, I was afraid, vague, and quickly changed the subject if I could. I hated icebreaker questions at a party. I was silent and a mystery to those wanting to learn more about me. I just did not know what to say. I had blocked memories of my early childhood.

My Rawa father, Papa Neyuro, was the first person to help me understand that unless I knew my past, I did not know who I was and who I am. I am glad God did not let me stay the unknown man.

In a dream, my friend Ken and I were at a sizeable car fair. I was to pick a car that I thought represented me. I could have any car I wanted, and money was not an issue. Ken said he would make it easy for me. All the vehicles disappeared except one. It was a fire-engine-red sports car of some type. It was glowing with brilliance: a brand-new Porsche.

When I woke up, I wondered why I could not choose and needed help. I told Ken about my dream, and he said the sports car represents my type of ministry, a one-on-one ministry.

In the past, I took on the identity given to me by others. I did not know I had distinguishing characteristics that made me uniquely me. I found out who I am and the kind of ministry I was to have, with Ken's help.

Crying for the First Time in Thirty-Eight Years

What am I to do with the considerable ache in my heart? My closest family or friends have betrayed me. I bear the scars that are painful yet. I shut my emotions down tight and did not cry for many years. I finally took the courage to seek help. My counselor read me like a book. I felt safe with him and eventually shared the abuse and shame. The dam holding my blocked feelings burst. I cried for the first time in thirty-eight years. It was as if I were holding my broken heart out to him. Please be gentle; I still hurt.

His healing words touched something profound. I am the Precious Moments figurine holding my broken heart in both hands. I have a tear on my cheek. There is a promise attached: "This, too, shall pass!" My emotions are free, and the broken heart is mended.

My Lament for My Father's Love

I long for your touch. I long for your affirmation. As a child, I longed for you to pick me up, cuddle me, and play with me. I wanted to greet you at the door when you came home from work each day. I longed for you to tell me you loved me. I longed for you to say you were proud of me.

Now your voice sounds angry and condemning. I dread when you come home from work. I know a spanking is coming. It is a trivial thing. You seem too busy to have time with me. You break your promises as quickly as you make them. When you look at me, I do not see your eyes light up. I act out to make you mad. I want to cause you pain.

Now I am a father. It is not easy being a father. I judged you harshly. Now Steve is judging me. I did not know you were like me. I did not know your dad was that way with you. No wonder you did not know how to be a father. You never had a father to teach you. Either he was too busy, or he did not care. You had no positive role model.

How do I learn how to relate to others? How do I learn how to solve problems? How do I show acceptance and love? How do I be a father without my father teaching me? What am I supposed to do? Who am I?

The Carousel

As a counselor, one watches for patterns. If you miss what is essential in a person's life, he will repeat the information. If it takes several times, that is all right. My memory marker is a carousel with a horse going around. A carousel with many-colored horses makes it easy to see the black one when it comes around. Watch for it. The presenting problem may be a smoke-screen for a more pressing issue. Listen to the person's story; the essential parts will keep coming around.

Surfing the Wave of the Holy Spirit

I realized control was a big part of my life. I lived in a fantasy world but was depressed and angry, not trusting others or myself. I visualized I was standing on the outside and watching life from a distance, not responding. I was frozen with fear, like the ostrich with its head in the sand, as I imagined a tsunami coming toward me. I was helpless. Not a tsunami to destroy; it was the Holy Spirit rushing to rescue me. The Holy Spirit gave me a surfboard so I could surf His wave. Safety and having fun are new experiences for me.

Twenty-Seven Years in Wycliffe

My wife and I were like bulldozers breaking new ground, preparing the Weri and Rawa to read their New Testaments. If people do not know how to read, they are locked away from God's Word. Literacy unlocks the Scripture by giving people the skills to read in their language.

Recent technology makes it possible for the translators to put the Bible onto solar-powered, pocket-sized players. A person does not need to be literate to hear the Scriptures in their language.

Martin Luther said, "I have held many things in my hands and lost them all; but whatever I have placed in God's hands, that I always possess."

If each page of the Scriptures talked, they would tell of extreme highs and lows and the roller-coaster rides the Bible translators experienced in the seven through forty years spent translating. There are several reasons for this:

A. How isolated the people are.

B. The level of education in the area.

C. How much time the translator is involved in the program. To the Weri and Rawa communities, many barriers hindered them from accepting the Scriptures.

The Story of the Bilum

One of the most useful items in Papua New Guinea is something called a bilum. It is a string bag. They come in many sizes and are used by both men and women. Women carry all sorts of things in their bilums: firewood, vegetables freshly dug from the garden, and even their babies! (They have a special bilum for a baby.) Little girls begin carrying small bilums when they are old enough to walk. By the time they are teenagers, their neck muscles have strengthened to the point that they can carry unimaginably huge loads. They can take several heavily loaded bilums at once, with the weight-bearing straps placed on their foreheads and the bag hanging on their backs.

Men carry a much smaller bilum with the strap around their neck, or over their shoulders. They usually contain personal items like betel nut, a white-powdered lime container which is a necessary complement to chewing betel nut, and some money. The bilum is tremendously useful.

But how does a bilum start? It begins as a piece of string, a bit of fiber. Women shred the leaves of individual plants into fibers and then roll several of these fibers into a string. Whenever they need more string, they make it on the spot, so it becomes one string without knots. Fiber from a plant, when twisted together with other fibers, creates a secure string. A single string, no matter how strong, cannot carry much. There must be many fibers woven together to make the string. Then they become useful.

The making of the bilum can be compared with the missionary work of the Wycliffe Bible translators. We are a team. By the team, I mean the translators, literacy workers who teach people to read, and a host of support workers: doctors, nurses, dentists, pilots, mechanics, electricians, printers, computer personnel, and many others. The other team members are the people at home, such as you, who give, pray, encourage, and show your love to us.

If we were each merely a fiber or even a whole string standing alone, we could never accomplish much. However, we can achieve beautiful things when we are woven together by God's hand into a team. The entire team carries the weight of Bible translation. None of the strings can boast they are taking more of a load than the others are. Thank you for being a fellow string with us in the goal of Bible translation.

The Rawa New Testament cover had a picture of a bilum hanging from a cross; inside the bilum was an open Bible. The bilum symbolized a person's heavy burden. The cross represented Jesus. The open Bible inside the bilum represented Matthew 11:28, "Come to Me, all who are weary and heavy-laden, and I will give you rest."

We Look on the Wrong Side of the Pattern

Corrie Ten Boom's story is told in the book The Hiding Place. For the first fifty years of her life, nothing at all out of the ordinary happened to her. She was an old-maid watchmaker living contentedly with her spinster sister and their elderly father in the tiny Dutch house over their shop. As regulated as their watches, their uneventful days revolved around their abiding love for one another. However, with the Nazi invasion and occupation of Holland, a story did ensue.

Corrie and her family became leaders in the Dutch Underground, hiding Jewish people in their home in a specially built room and aiding their escape from the Nazis. For their help, all but Corrie found death in a concentration camp. The Hiding Place is their story.

In her talks, she showed the backside of a tapestry to the audience, the one with all the threads. This side had no pattern and no beauty. But when she turned it over, one could see a lovely crown.

God is behind the scenes in all our stories. His hand holds the shuttle; His foot is on the treadle. According to His divine design, he will weave the web of our life into a beautiful and glorious pattern.

Corrie ten Boom expressed her thoughts about life in her poem, "Weaver."

"My life is but a weaving between my God and me. I cannot choose the colors.

He weaves steadily. Oft He weaves sorrow, and I in foolish pride, forget He sees the upper, and I the underside.

Not till the loom is silent, and the shuttles cease to fly, will God unroll the canvas and reveal the reason why.

The dark threads are as needful in the weaver's skillful hand as the threads of gold and silver in the pattern He has planned.

He knows; He loves; He cares; nothing this truth can dim. He gives the very best to those who leave the choice to Him."

This poem powerfully spoke to me and reminded me life consists of good and bad times. Knowing Christ and having His Word in our hearts is the only way Christians can face missionary work's daily challenges without defeat.

God said, "It is Time to Begin Again"

Dudley Stiles was a highly successful stockbroker. He was a Christian, yet he did not practice honest business. He was caught dealing in rapidly buying and selling skyscrapers in the greater Dallas area. He went to jail and served his time.

Dudley loved singing and had a deep tenor voice. God did a deep cleansing of his life, and Dudley composed and sang many beautiful songs. He composed a beautiful song about seeing the day dawning, and as the sun warms the earth, he feels God's gift of the new birth. He hears God say, "It's okay to begin again."

Shortly thereafter, I came home from serving the Lord in Papua New Guinea. I was lost and afraid of God. I did not know who I was or what kind of work I would do. I began thinking I had failed as a missionary, a husband, and a father. Was there anything I could do without messing up? I wondered if more things would come back to beat me down. I cycled in endless spirals of chaos, lost hope, and woe-is-me parties. I had no desire to live and often thought of suicide.

Then I heard Dudley Stiles sing "Begin Again" on the radio. This song spoke so profoundly to my heart that I could not forget it. Sometime later, Dudley Stiles had a concert in the Dallas area, and I attended.

Significantly few things have affected me so much as "Begin Again." It is time to begin again with God and watch my new dreams grow. Nothing is too bold when I begin with God. After the storm, begin again. I see my rainbow; I see the sunshine; I hear the birds sing again; so, I begin again. It is okay to begin with God and watch my new dreams grow.

Dr. Sydney, this song is on YouTube, and I want you to hear it. It is my favorite song. Listen to Mr. Stiles' clear, resonating, tenor voice and the powerful lyrics.

A New Start for Me

When personal tragedy broke me, it allowed God's changes to begin. In the chaos, God saw something beautiful in me. He provided me the opportunity for a fresh start. I humbled myself before God and gladly gave Him my all.

His spark of hope flickered into a flame in my heart. I could only stand still and watch the newness grow. I began to dream and visualize change happening to me. Some things scared me and yet excited me at the same time. God began to make bold hope come forth from weak faith. When I stopped interfering, God gave me bold new dreams. Nothing is impossible with God when I get out of His way. Nothing is too bold, and I can achieve the impossible dream.

Nothing is impossible when God is in control. Nothing is too bold when I begin with God. My new day has begun, and I am refreshed. It is a brand-new day; everything is so fresh. I will begin with God; there is no better way to start my day as I watch my new dreams grow.

God took my life, and through His mercy and grace, is using me to show the world how deeply He loves and cares. We see this through the tangled course of my life from birth, which will continue until I die. I look back over the years and see these reminders. I reflect and remember, and now I praise God.

DR. SYDNEY: I have a surprise for you. I know how much you thought of Dark Pony. When I was a little boy, my mother read a children's book, Dark Pony. It is out of print, but I found the story with pictures on the internet. I made a copy for you. Sit back, and I will read it to you. This copy is for you.

"At night Dark Pony came running along the road. At night he took many children to Sleepy Town. Every night his four little feet came galloping,

galloping. His color was dark, and he came just in the dark. So that is why the children called him Dark Pony.

"One night a boy met Dark Pony running along the road. The little boy called, 'Please take me down to Sleepy Town.' Dark Pony stopped running. Up jumped the little boy, and away they went. Galloping, galloping, galloping!

"Soon they met a little girl. The little girl called, 'Please take me down to Sleepy Town.' Dark Pony stopped running, and the girl jumped up behind the boy. 'Go, go, Dark Pony!' she said. And away they went! Galloping, galloping, galloping.

"Then they met a little puppy running along the road. The little puppy sat up and called, 'Bow-wow, bow-wow!' Dark Pony stopped, and the puppy jumped up behind the girl. 'Go, go Dark Pony,' they said. And away they went. Galloping, galloping, galloping!

"Next, they met a little gray squirrel; he sat up in the road and called, 'Please take me too.'

"Jump up. Jump up behind me," said the puppy. So, the little gray squirrel jumped up behind the puppy. And away they went galloping along the road to Sleepy Town. Galloping, galloping, galloping! Faster and faster and faster!

"Happy children sang and sang. The faster they went, the faster they sang. Soon Dark Pony began to go slower. The puppy, the squirrel, the boy, and the girl were all very sleepy. Dark Pony was sleepy too. Slower and slower and slower and slower he went; at last, he stopped. He had come to Sleepy Town; so, had the puppy, the squirrel, the boy, and the girl. All five had come to Sleepy Town."

Jerry: Thank you. You have given me a new meaning for Dark Pony. This is a beautiful story, and Little Jerry Wayne and I will cherish and share it with our grandchildren. Ben is going to love it.

Session 22—Closing

Dr. Sydney: I am so glad God brought you here. For both of us, this whole counseling experience has been an exciting journey with God. We have accomplished our goal of seeing you become healthy. Now it is time to say goodbye. I will sum up our journey with two words: Bravo, Lord!

Please stand as I pray and give you a blessing. Do you mind if I place my hand on your shoulder as I give you this blessing? I will pray for you.

Jerry: Please do.

Dr. Sydney: Heavenly Father, you are so good. May you receive honor and glory from Jerry's memory markers. We praise you for the deep work you are doing in his life, in Jesus's name. There are so many places Jerry can now look back on as victory mileposts. Thank you for letting me be a part of the excellent work you are doing in his life.

Jerry may God pour out such a blessing of His presence on you that you cannot contain it but instead must leak, spill, and overflow with His goodness, grace, and love. May every place trying to hinder you in fulfilling your call and destiny be destroyed and turned into a highway of holiness that you walk on in joy and abundance. May the lost spiritual inheritance of any of your generations be recovered and prosper in you and all your descendants for a thousand generations. May you be a glory-filled ambassador for the kingdom of God, one whose life brings praise and glory to our Lord and God Almighty.[57] Shalom. Jerry. Go with God.

Postscript

Update

Dr. Minirth of the Minirth-Meier Clinic personally forgave us a debt of $50,000. After two months, Dr. Minirth recommended I place Steve in a Christian residential-treatment ranch. I chose HeartLight Ministries near Longview, Texas, about two hours' drive from Dallas, where he could receive the help we were unable to give him.

Steve was there for about fifteen months, but he sabotaged himself at the ranch. For bad behavior and disrespecting authority, the leaders kicked Steve out of the program, and Steve had no place to go. We had not yet healed enough for him to come home. His only option was to return to HeartLight, apologize, and see if they would take him back. He did. He was required to sleep in the barn until the staff noticed a change in him, and then he could move back into the house. Eventually he earned his way back inside.

After several months of relatively good behavior, Steve acted out again and was kicked out without hope of returning. We didn't feel ready to take him back home but had no choice. Once he was home, I called a family meeting to discuss what to do with Steve. We drafted a family constitution regarding what was acceptable behavior and the consequences for misbehavior. I told him bluntly if he hurt anyone, I was calling the police, and they could take him to jail, and we wouldn't bail him out. Steve tested me once by overstaying his weekend curfew.

Steve saw a change of attitude in me and a willingness to understand him, and I saw a change in him, as well. I enjoyed this new relationship with my son, and it was a joy having him home. He lived with us for several years and began Duncanville High School's Advertising Design program. He started earning A's, and two of his designs won first place in the Texas State competition. After graduation, Steve joined the U.S. Navy, where he did well. One day his supervisor mentioned to Steve that his daughter was interested in him. A few years later, they got married and had a son named Christopher.

God took our broken family and put it back together again. That, too, was teamwork. We did our work, others did theirs, and God did His part. It was a miracle of love and grace.

We learned a lot about crucial things in life. Our relationship with God is the most important. Our relationship with each other as a family is second, and our work for God is next. God made us who we are and placed us where we are. We choose how we respond to God and others and what we do with where we are.

"Blessed be the God and Father of our Lord Jesus Christ, the Father of mercies and God of all comfort, who comforts us in all our affliction so that we will be able to comfort those in any affliction with the comfort with which we are comforted by God" (2 Corinthians 1:3–4).

When speaking at churches or with friends, I couldn't say all was well. I could only talk about my difficult journey with God. I was no longer angry with God and could talk about what was happening right then with He and I. I mentioned the books I found helpful. I discovered many of the people I spoke with had gone through similar family problems. I would mention the significant number of medical problems we were facing, simply asking for prayer.

It seemed all roads for returning to PNG were closed. Five of our main supporting churches told us they did not want to support us as home-assigned missionaries and would drop our support if we did not return to the field. The recurring question was, "When would we return to PNG?" I said we didn't know.

"You will make known to me the path of life; In Your presence is fullness of joy; In Your right hand, there are pleasures forever" (Psalm 16:11).

MEMORIAL TO THE LORD

My Ebenezer—Commemorations of Divine Assistance

MEMORIAL STONES IN THE BIBLE—ETERNAL WALL OF ANSWERED PRAYER

There is a biblical precedent for laying stones as a memorial to the Lord to remember the good things He has done for us. Eternal Wall takes inspiration from these monuments and their significance.

At least three biblical characters are laying memorial stones, and these become significant locations throughout history. Bethel is where Jacob memorialized his vision. Gilgal is where Joshua commemorated the Israelites' miraculous entrance into the Promised Land. Samuel erects an Ebenezer stone after God thwarts the Philistine's attack.

Eternal Wall is in many ways replicating these biblical memorial stones, as we glorify God with a national monument of 1 million bricks, with each brick symbolizing an answered prayer.

- It is our hope to:

- Reignite faith in God

- Remind us of what He has done before

- Create an atmosphere of worship

- Increase our confidence in Jesus

Bethel

The first biblical reference to memorial stones comes in Genesis 28:10–22 when Jacob set a pillar in Bethel to commemorate a powerful vision of God that he experienced while sleeping there. The experience was so striking that Jacob felt it must be commemorated, so he erected the stone upon which he slept.

Jacob did not want to forget what God had given him. Bethel, meaning 'House of God,' then became an important center for worship. By physically remembering what God had done, Jacob increased his faith and the faith of those who later worshiped there.

Gilgal

In Joshua 4:1–8, God commands the Israelites to cross the Jordan River, which He has miraculously stopped. Joshua leads the twelve tribes to remove boulders from the riverbed, which they erect in the Promised Land in a place called Gilgal. These twelve stones of Jordan were a memorial to God's love and miraculous assistance.

These stones are appreciated not just by those who witnessed the miracle. Joshua 4:21–22 explains that "In the future, your children will ask, 'What do these stones mean?' Then you can tell them, 'This is where the Israelites crossed the Jordan on dry ground.'" God longs for us to proclaim His goodness to future generations.

The remembrance stones in Gilgal reminded future generations of the God of miracles so that their faith would be renewed. We believe that Eternal Wall will do this as it memorializes Jesus for centuries.

Ebenezer

In the Old Testament, 1 Samuel 7:7–12 depicts the Israelites under imminent attack from the Philistines. God leads them to victory, so Samuel erects a large stone and names it Ebenezer, meaning "the stone of help." Samuel recognized the source of their victory and publicly declared it. It ensured that the Israelites would not forget God's grace by permanently commemorating His goodness. The memorial stones made sure all glory went to God, the illustrator of Israel's success.

Photos

crabgrass

praying mantis

Eagle and the Turkey

Teddy Bear Little Jerry Wayne

The Old Wooden Plank

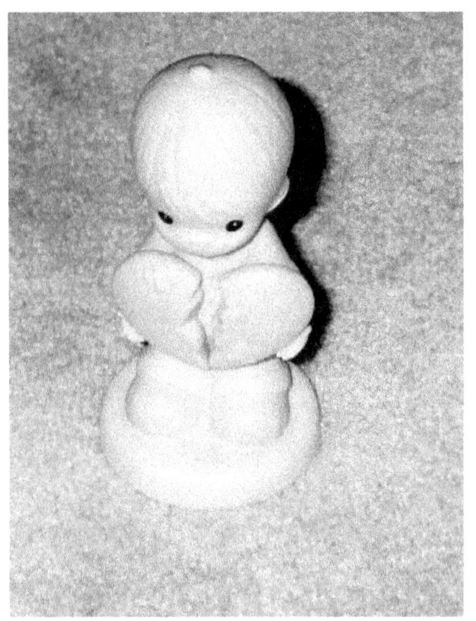

New Identity

Surfing the holy Spirit

Carousel

Precious Moments—Crying for the
first time in 38 years

Robby, the seal
My Air Force friends called me Robby, and most of the time I walked with my shoulders slumped and head down. Larry saw a toy leopard seal in a shop; its name tag said "Robby." He bought it, gave it to me, and said, "Whenever you get discouraged, think of Robby with its head held high."

He said I was a child of the king. A prince does not go around with his head hanging down; no prince walks like that. Hold your head high and stand up tall. Look at Robby; his head is held high.

The Bulldozer

Preparing the way for the Weri and Rawa to read their New Testaments. I thought I myself as a bulldozer leveling the playing field, removing the barriers for the Weri and Rawa people through literacy and community development.

There would be no Rawa Literacy Program without Jerry, Yunu, and Neyuro (Ne-yu-ro).

The first-ever Rawa prep-school class. I am so proud of these children. The first-time children ever read anything in their mother-tongue language—a great day for The Rawa people

Steve and Jerry, 1994

THE END.

Endnotes

1 Thank you for your request to use the NASB in your work. Permission for your project has been granted and is in the attached file. Code:--IP:-75.21.251.47-mlist:-No-

2 Board of Licensed Professional Counselors and Therapists ... https://www.oregon.gov/OBLPCT/Pages/CE.aspx

3 Board of Licensed Professional Counselors and Therapists ... https://www.oregon.gov/OBLPCT/Pages/CE.aspx

4 Dr. Sydney is fiction, so is Mountain Brook; the counseling sessions are fiction but realistic. Dr. Gilliam is real; he is permitted to use his material. The storyline is authentic and accurately represents the process of counseling using the models of the inner child and the landmarks, boundaries, and walls. I am the client and am real; my life events presented in the counseling sessions are my biography. Some names and details are changed to protect the persons.

Elzy Wood, a family friend, permitted me to use his picture as Dr. Sydney.

5 Board of Licensed Professional Counselors and Therapists ... https://www.oregon.gov/OBLPCT/Pages/CE.aspx

6 What is professional counseling? https://www.counseling.org/aca-community/learn-about-counseling

7 WAC 246-810-031: https://app.leg.wa.gov/WAC/default.aspx?cite=246-810-031

8 Dayspring Counseling Services—Counseling from the ... https://dayspringcounseling.org

I applied Dr. Gilliam's credentials to Dr. Sydney

9 The Counseling Process The Professional Counselor
https://www.sulross.edu/sites/default/files//sites/default/files/

10 Inner child therapy is based on the premise that people emotionally struggle because they have unresolved childhood issues. In this psychotherapy method, the therapist guides the client through an in-depth exploration of childhood traumatic events and directs the client in reworking the associated disturbing emotions.

11 What is professional counseling?
https://www.counseling.org/aca-community/learn-about-counseling

12 Wycliffe Bible Translators | Christian Mission
https://www.wycliffe.org
The Summer Institute of Linguistics, Wycliffe Bible
https://constantinereport.com/the-summer-institute-of-linguistics
The two-sided mission organization comprising Wycliffe Bible Translators and the Summer Institute of Linguistics is a paradox that begs for an explanation. The Summer Institute has long been doing laudable linguistic, humanitarian work in many countries, while Wycliffe has been one of the largest, fastest growing, and most controversial Christian missionary enterprises in the world.

13 WAC 246-810-031:
http://apps.leg.wa.gov/WAC/default.aspx?cite=246-810-031
RAF Alconbury
https://www.rafalconbury.com

The 423d Force Support Squadron is responsible for providing an enhanced quality-of-life, facilities, and programs for military, civilian and dependents in the RAF Alconbury and RAF Molesworth communities.

14 The Navigators is a worldwide Christian para-church organization headquartered in Colorado Springs, Colorado. Its purpose is the discipling of Christians with a particular emphasis on enabling them to share their faith with others. The organization's calling statement is "to advance the Gospel

of Jesus and His Kingdom into the nations through spiritual generations of laborers living and discipling among the lost."

15 Informed Consent for Therapy Services—Adult | Center for https://centerforethicalpractice.org/ethical-legal-resources/practice

16 The Keys to Rewarding Relationships: Secure Attachment ... *https://www.psychologytoday.com/us/blog/the...*

17 https://en.wikipedia.org/wiki/The_Pilgrim's_Progress
First Part
The entire book is presented as a dream sequence narrated by an omniscient narrator. The allegory's protagonist, Christian, is an everyman character, and the plot canters o…
Second Part
The Second Part of The Pilgrim's Progress presents the pilgrimage of Christian's wife, Christiana, and their sons, and the maiden, Mercy. They visit the same stopping places the…

18 Hinds' Feet on High Places Summary & Study Guide www.bookrags.com/studyguide-hinds-feet-on-high-places

Hinds' Feet on High Places by Hannah Hurnard is a highly allegorical novel that traces the steps of the main character, Much Afraid, from a frightened, deformed, lost soul to a beautiful, spiritually connected, joyful being. Throughout …

19 My professor from seminary

20 The Road Not Taken by Robert Frost | Poe… *poemanalysis.com/robert-frost/the-road-not-taken/*

21 Unlocking the Mysteries of the Human Heart | The Institute for Creation Research (icr.org) Unlocking the Mysteries of the Human Heart By Henry M. Morris III, D. Min. *
*Dr. Morris is Chief Executive Officer of the Institute for Creation Research. Cite this article: Morris III, H. 2008. Unlocking the Mysteries of the Human Heart. Acts & Facts. 37 (2): 4.

22 Dr. Gilliam, Little Flock Ministries

23 Dr. Gilliam, Little Flock Ministries

24 Dr. Larry Gilliam, Reparenting the Inner Child Reparenting: Volume 1: Gilliam, Dr. Larry: 9781632320582

https://www.amazon.com/Reparenting-1-Dr-Larry-Gilliam/dp/1632320584
Reparenting: Volume 1 [Gilliam, Dr. Larry] on Amazon.com. *FREE* shipping on qualifying offers. Reparenting: Volume 1
Reparenting: Volume 2: Dr. Larry Gilliam: 9781632321879 ...
https://www.christianbook.com/reparenting-volume-2-larry-gilliam/9781632321879/pd/321879
Reparenting: Volume 2 (9781632321879) by Dr. Larry Gilliam. Search by title, catalog stock #, author, ISBN, etc. New Year's Sale—thru 1/4

25 THINGS YOU SHOULD KNOW ABOUT HOW GOD SEES YOU By Jack Kelley Wednesday October 21st, 2020, About 11 Minutes to Read

26 The four stages of anger: the buildup
balancedlifeskills.com/2010/04/05/the-four-stages-of-ang…

27 The Integrated Approach—Restoring the Foundations
https://www.restoringthefoundations.org/integrated-approach

28 Dislodging Negative Entity Attachments|*wakeupworld.com/2015/10/04/dislodging-negative*

29 Infants process faces long before they recognize other ...
https://news.stanford.edu/news/2012/december/infants-proce

30 Binaural Beats—Attachment and Trauma Treatment Centre ...
https://www.attachment-and-trauma-treatment-centre-for-heali

31 Why is body language so important?
https://hospitalityinsights.ehl.edu/body-language-important

32 What is Emotion Regulation? …
positivepsychology.com/emoti…

33 Environmental and emotional triggers that control your ...
https://scottabelfitness.com/environmental-and-emotional-t

34 Overcome-Self-Sabotage-Workbook.pdf (gemmastone.org)

35 Clarity of Purpose and How to Attain it
www.successconsciousness.com/blog/goal-setting/cl…

36 Author of The Pursuit of Purpose: How God Leads You Into His Perfect Will (2019) 7 Ways to Guard Your Heart | Before The Cr…

www.beforethecross.com/biblical-teachings/7-ways-to-gu…

37 7 Ways to Guard Your Heart | Before The Cr…
www.beforethecross.com/biblical-teachings/7-ways-to-gu…

38 https://iblp.org/questions/how-can-i-reclaim-areas-my-life-i-surrendered-satan

39 A Woman Scorned—Deborah's Arise!
womeninleadershipblog.wordpress.com/2016/08/14/…

40 Ligonier Ministries 421 Ligonier Court Sanford, FL 32771, by emailing us at webmaster@ligonier.org, or by calling 800-435-4343.
41 Root of Bitterness
https://www.greatbiblestudy.com/physical-healing/root-of-bitt

42 John Owen: Nature, Power, Deceit, and Prevalence of the ...
https://www.ccel.org/ccel/owen/indwellingsin.i.vii.html

43 The Navigators—Life-to-Life Discipleshiphttps://www.navigators.org Apr 26, 2021 · The Navigators® is an international, interdenominational Christian ministry established in 1933. Our motto is, "To know Christ, make Him known, and help others do the same®." We do this through building Life …

44 10 Negative Thoughts We All Have and What to Think Instead (lifehack.org)

45 10 Negative Thoughts We All Have and What to Think Instead (lifehack.org)

46 People's Bible Notes for Romans 5:8.

47 www.kingjamesbibleonline.org/Romans-5-8/

48 How to Manage Estranged Children—Reconcile Parent Child Relationship (empoweringparents.com)

49 Janet Christensen introduced this phrase to the group

50 Mental health of children and parents —a strong connection https://www.cdc.gov/childrensmentalhealth/features/menta

51 Simple Ways to Boost Your Child's Self-Esteem | Parents www.parents.com/toddlers-preschoolers/developmen…

52 Bachelor of Arts in Child Development | UAGC | University of Arizona Global Campus

53 Why the Pharisees Could Not Recognize the Lord Jesus Was … https://www.testifygod.org/pharisees-could-not-recognize-M

54 Self Perception—How we perceive ourselves is based on our self beliefs (authentic-self.com)

55 Fear Dreams: What Are They Trying To Tell You? | HuffPost Life

56 Fear Dreams: What Are They Trying To Tell You? | HuffPost Life

57 By Sylvia Engle

www.ingramcontent.com/pod-product-compliance
Lightning Source LLC
Chambersburg PA
CBHW051448050726
47593CB00005B/1974